INTELLIGENT READING

Intelligent Reading

B. W. M. Young, M.A.

HEADMASTER OF CHARTERHOUSE

P. D. R. Gardiner, M.A.

SENIOR ENGLISH MASTER, CHARTERHOUSE

LONGMAN

LONGMAN GROUP LIMITED
London

Associated companies, branches and representatives
throughout the world

© Longman Group Ltd 1964

First published 1964
Fourteenth impression 1978

ISBN 0 582 32603 6

Printed in Hong Kong by
Commonwealth Printing Press Ltd

Contents

† This sign indicates an extract only.

CONTENTS

CONTENTS

Acknowledgements

We are grateful to the following for permission to include copyright material:

George Allen & Unwin Ltd. for material from *Fear, Punishment, Anxiety and the Wolfenden Report* by Charles Berg; Edward Arnold (Publishers) Ltd. for material from *Two Cheers for Democracy* by E. M. Forster; BBC Publications for material from the Introduction to 'The Problem of Suffering' by Margaret E. Rose; the author and the Clarendon Press for material from *Two Concepts of Liberty* by Sir Isaiah Berlin; the author and The Critical Quarterly Society for 'Restoration of Gender' by Francis Berry; the author for material from *Repair the Ruins* by Harry Blamires; Cambridge University Press for material from *Dilemmas* by Gilbert Ryle; the author and the author's agents, Curtis Brown Ltd., for material from *A Fearful Joy* by Joyce Cary published by Michael Joseph Ltd.; Chatto and Windus Ltd. for material from *The Uses of Literacy* by Richard Hoggart; Constable & Co. Ltd. for material from *Hardy the Novelist* by Lord David Cecil; Gerald Duckworth & Co. Ltd. for material from *Man, Morals and Society* by J. C. Flugel; Faber and Faber Ltd. for 'In Time of War, VIII' from *Collected Shorter Poems* by W. H. Auden, for part of 'Lay your sleeping head, my love' from *Another Time* by W. H. Auden, for material from *Notes towards the Definition of Culture* by T. S. Eliot and for 'A Street in Cumberland' from *Rock Face* by Norman Nicholson; Harcourt, Brace & World, Inc. for 'Nine Birds . . .' from *Poems 1923–1954* by E. E. Cummings, copyright 1950 by E. E. Cummings; George G. Harrap & Co. Ltd. for material from *The Boundaries of Science* by Magnus Pyke; Hutchinson & Co. (Publishers) Ltd. for material from *The State and the Citizen* by J. D. Mabbott; James Nisbet and Company, Limited for material from *The Doctrine of Atonement* by Leonard Hodgson; the author for material from an article on African Independence by Roland Oliver published in *The Listener*, 7 February 1963; the Estate of George Orwell and A. M. Heath & Company Ltd. for material from 'The Prevention of Literature' from *Selected Essays* by George Orwell; Oxford University Press for material from *Rehabilitation and Other Essays* by C. S. Lewis and from *The Individual and the Universe* by A. C. B. Lovell; Penguin Books Ltd. for material from *Know Your Own I.Q.* by H. J. Eysenck, from *Introduction to Modern Architecture* by J. M. Richards, from *Philosophy and the Physicists* by Susan Stebbing, from *Britain in the Sixties – Education for To-morrow* by John Vaizey and from *The Scientific Attitude* by C. H. Waddington; Sir Isaac Pitman & Sons Ltd. for material from *Glaucon* by M. V. C. Jeffreys; Laurence Pollinger Ltd. and the Estate of the Late Mrs. Frieda Lawrence for material from *Reflections on the Death of a Porcupine* by D. H. Lawrence published by William Heinemann Ltd.; the Public Trustee for material from *Music Ho!* by Constant Lambert; the Public Trustee and The Society of Authors for material from *The Doctor's Dilemma* by George Bernard Shaw; *The Spectator* for a review by Ronald Bryden from *The Spectator*, 6 July 1962 and for an article by Katharine Whitehorn from *The Spectator*, 19 October 1962; the author for material from 'Confession is Good for Ideas' by J. W. N. Watkins published in *The Listener*, 18 April 1963; C. A. Watts & Co. Ltd. for material from 'Wordsworth in the Tropics' from *Do What You Will* by Aldous Huxley; George Weidenfeld and Nicolson Ltd. for material from *No Further West* by Dan Jacobson; *The Sunday Times* for three Problems by B. W. M. Young; Longmans, Green & Co. Ltd. for material from *English Social History* by G. M. Trevelyan; the Executors of H. G. Wells for material from *Kipps* by H. G. Wells. The authors also wish to thank Miss H. M. Adams of the Department of Education, Edinburgh University, for rousing, and guiding, their interest in the setting of 'multiple choice' questions on a passage of English.

Introduction

Polonius: What do you read, my lord?
Hamlet: Words, words, words.
Polonius: What is the matter, my lord?

It is said repeatedly – indeed it is becoming a cliché of our time – that sixth-formers are less skilful at writing reasoned and serviceable English than they should be; that the skill is an essential one, not only for passing examinations; and that boys and girls would be better at writing if only they were better at reading. Television and the telephone are usually blamed for this: watching, hearing, and speaking, valuable in themselves, steal time from the harder means of communication – closely-argued page of print and recalcitrant pen. It is also said that, in a world of headlines and snap judgments, the serious ideas that are the basis of all good writing are unfamiliar to young minds; thus, even when there is fluency, it is all too often wasted on platitudes and wordy padding. 'Nothing to say, and no idea of how to say it' is the verdict of many examiners – as no doubt it always has been.

All this is true. Those of us who try to teach English to sixth-formers have long known that it is not an easy task – even before universities began to tell us how inadequately we do it, and to set special papers to prove their point. Three or four periods a week are not a large allowance for training boys to read intelligently and to write lucidly and accurately; indeed most of us spend a lifetime learning these skills for ourselves. Yet something can be done: and many a sixth-form teacher feels that it could be done more effectively if only he could lay hands on the right book to help him in his task. *Intelligent Reading* is two schoolmasters' idea of the kind of book they themselves would like, to supplement what they say in class, or write on the blackboard, or utter as comment while they return essays individually.

The main features we required from a book were these:

1. *Passages of argument, both cool and passionate, in which modern writers deal with topics of general importance.*

To imagine, to observe, to describe, and to relate are arts

that can be studied in fiction – or in articles which give a plain factual account of a simple matter; but to argue coherently and clearly on controversial topics is something that students learn much less easily from their normal reading. The ideas themselves, the way in which they are marshalled, the relevance of examples, the style that makes a point telling – all these should be studied in concentration if a book is to help sixth-formers to write essays on serious themes. So our extracts show a range of modern writers developing ideas and conveying them to the reader in a variety of ways. The reader is then encouraged, sometimes by further passages of argument, sometimes by extracts of fiction or poetry, sometimes by questions, to look more closely both at the ideas and at the writer's method of expounding them. If one weakness in students' essay-writing is a lack of ideas on serious subjects, this book can be regarded in some measure as an anthology to stir up thought.

2. *Opportunities to trace connexions between school subjects and first-hand experience.*

Students tend to keep their various subjects in separate files of the cabinet. Yet, however much the intellectual disciplines of each subject may differ, it is surely a necessity of education to trace their connexions and to understand, at least in part, their conflicts. Moreover there is a second danger – particularly for those who study hard out of a sense of duty or ambition but are not deeply interested in the work of the classroom – that academic subjects should be held distinct from everyday experience, as though they were rarefied or theoretical. What the pupil learns in the classroom or writes in an essay shows him intellectually on his best behaviour – a state that may be tenuously related to his response, say, to a football match or a television programme. We have tried to erode these two types of barrier, partly by including passages that attack the same topics from different directions, and partly by enlarging the scope of each passage; the reader is invited to extend an author's argument to the context of another topic or of his own experience. Thus by watching the scientist grapple with the poet, or the psychologist with the theologian, and by testing an idea on his own social or school life, the student may be lured out of academic ruts.

3. *An incentive to read perceptively, grasping the points made by the writer and seeing his shades of meaning.*

Failing to read at all may be the main enemy; but reading superficially and skimming along the surface of some close-packed prose is a real danger too. The great merit of a précis is that it compels one to penetrate to what is important; this discipline we wanted to extend in various ways, providing the student with a chance of correcting his own précis here and there. For, although the *expression* of ideas is hard to improve without a teacher's help, *understanding* can be learnt on one's own – more effectively, perhaps, than by gazing with disappointment or apathy at a returned précis, covered with red ink.

4. *Some emphasis on the fact that there are right and wrong answers to a question in English, as in other subjects.*

Too often sixth-form English seems to the student a subjective matter. He has little means of discovering whether his reading of a passage has been intelligent or shallow, and praise or blame from a master often comes in general terms. By contrast, his work in his specialist subject seems to him to be objectively assessed: he knows what his weaknesses are, and what kind of work he must do on his own to remedy them. One way of helping the student to see how well or ill he reads is to devise questions which have a direct answer – and give the answer. Though this method has its dangers (indeed, the short answer is anathema to some teachers of English), we believe it has great value not only as a test but also as an exercise. We have therefore included a number of questions of this type. Where our answers, dogmatically given, are thought to be wrong, this may well be the starting-point of useful discussion in class; where they are generally agreed to be the right ones, those who differ can learn much (including humility) from trying to see why. To avoid the obvious danger – that a reader will unwittingly see the next answer before he has even considered the next question – we have 'scrambled' the answers by attaching numbers to questions in a random order but printing these numbers in sequence against the answers.

5. *A means of securing more written work from students without increasing the burden of corrections on the teacher.*

Even if a teacher gives three hours a week out of school

to correcting the work of pupils whom he sees for three hours in school, he is likely to find that he makes them write less (both in and out of school) than he would wish. Oral work leaves less aftermath – but it tends also to exercise a few of the brighter spirits, at the expense of those who most need continual exercise in thinking and writing. There are some things in English work, such as writing a sustained essay, which need all the time that a teacher can find for out-of-school correcting and for the individual returning of work; there are others, such as exercise in reading intelligently, which need not occupy the teacher, when he corrects, for nearly as long as they occupied the student. We have therefore laid emphasis on written work which the teacher can correct quickly (or the pupil can correct for himself); the object is not to provide more leisure for the teacher but to use time more fully for each pupil in a class.

One more point may be added: though the book is primarily intended for use in schools, we have also borne in mind the needs of those who will be reading on their own. For an interest in serious writing often develops when formal schooling is over, and we believe that there are many adults who would like to study the expression of ideas but do not know where to begin. We hope that this selection of pieces and the possibility of checking the answers to some of the questions may render this book useful to those who are teaching themselves.

These then are the special needs that prompted the making of this book: they were needs of students, but we hope and believe they are needs of many who have left school behind them. Its plan will readily be seen: short single passages come first, and later passages are grouped together because they have a similar theme – though often a very different view-point. All are thought by us to be of interest, in their ideas and their form, and to suggest discussion and thought about subjects that matter.

NOTE TO THE READER

The numbered questions are those to which answers are given
at the end of the book.

These numbers appear in *a random order* when the questions
are asked, but in the answers they are printed in the right order.
So, if you wish to check your own answer immediately you have
given it, you are less likely to glimpse the answer to the following question as well.

1 Health

† *The State and the Citizen*, by J. D. Mabbott, 1948

I take it without argument that disease is evil and health is good.
Until recently health was not a State concern. Each man pur-
sued it for himself. He could get a doctor to help him, if he could
afford it. He could combine voluntarily with other individuals
for treatment or exercise, if he could afford it. Voluntary
societies, from charitable or benevolent motives, might help to
bring health to those who had not got it and could not afford to
pay. Why did the State suddenly enter this field? It was not
merely that some people were too poor to afford doctors and,
10 unaided by any benevolent association, were neglected and
diseased. This might have justified greater activity by the benevolent and its extension on non-sectarian lines to all deserving
cases, but it would not have made health necessarily a State
concern. It was not merely that the cash nexus gave the whole
medical profession an interest, not in keeping people well, but in
keeping them ill, with the inevitable evils of unnecessary operations, treatment determined by the patient's purse and so on.
This might have been met by rising standards of professional
conduct, and an extension of the readiness, already widely
20 found in country practices, to do good work for the poor for
little or nothing.

No doubt these methods could never have entirely removed
the abuses nor given the poor any real chance of efficient attention or adequate treatment. But there was one factor which
made State action in medicine more than an attempt to protect
the rich hypochondriac from exploitation or the poor patient
from neglect and inefficiency. This factor was the germ theory
of disease, with the consequent recognition that no man can by

his own efforts achieve health in an unhealthy community, that
30 my own health is endangered unless my neighbour is compelled
to keep his premises sanitary and to isolate his infectious cases.
It is endangered also if those things which I cannot supply for
myself – gas, water and roads – are not kept clean. Just as no
individual and no voluntary association can prevent murder
and insecurity, so neither of these can control the incidence of
plague or typhoid or diphtheria. Freedom from disease can be
achieved only by State action. The methods to be adopted must
be judged by practical evidence and are no concern of political
philosophy.

40 Three of the possible methods have already been tried in this
country: (i) control of private persons (doctors and patients) by
regulation, as in the case of infectious disease; (ii) the working
of private persons (doctors and patients) into a national system,
as with the Insurance Acts; and (iii) the employment of State
doctors, as with the Medical Officer of Health. The relative
merits of these three methods, the division of the care of health
between them, and the proper development of any one at the
expense of the others cannot be determined by any theoretical
discussion. All that political theory can do is to lay bare the
50 necessary connection between the germ theory and State action,
and to leave detailed application to statesmen and scientists.

In the above discussion I have to some extent confused the
issue by treating 'health' and 'freedom from disease' as equivalent terms. Recent developments in this country have brought
out very clearly that there is here a distinction of principle. Has
the State a duty to promote health in a positive way as well as
to prevent disease? This seems to me far less certain. The duty
of the State would seem here to rest on the fact that, unless
facilities for the positive pursuit of health are State-provided,
60 some people will have no access to them at all (whereas in the
case of infectious disease, unless State action is taken, not only
some but all citizens are threatened). There are arguments by
which the interest of all in the positive health of some might be
defended. It is obviously to my interest that my poor neighbour
should not have typhoid. Is it to my interest that my poor
neighbour should have a playing-field, which I shall not use
but for which I shall pay? It may be said that I may want my
poor neighbour to fight for me, or with me, for my home, and

2

that he will fight better if he is fit. This has no doubt been
70 a powerful motive in countries whose governments have
regarded war as desirable, or as the main objective of national
organization. But anyone who regarded war as a necessary evil
would have to regard any expenditure on physical fitness, incurred with this ultimate object only, as a necessary evil also.
This 'security' argument is therefore inadequate.

It may be said that my neighbour will be less cost to me if he
has his playing field than if he does not. For he will be more fit
and the other work of the public health authorities will be
lessened and made less expensive. But once again I think the
80 ordinary man would feel that this was a sophism and would not
expect his contribution to public health to diminish in proportion to his increased contribution to national fitness. For he
knows that the enemy is so vast and so insidious that no gain in
in one place would really justify retrenchment in another. This
'economy' argument is therefore inadequate also.

But if these arguments are immoral, like the war argument,
or sophistical, like its alternatives, there is nothing left to which
we can appeal but the simple principles of benevolence or
justice. Yet why should the exercise of these virtues be State-
90 organized or made compulsory by an addition to our rates
or taxes? Why should benevolence or justice be exercised on
behalf of our fellow-citizens in particular? The answer to the
latter question is that, while justice and benevolence should not
be so limited, our fellow-citizens have a prior claim upon us, on
the principle defended above that membership of an association
creates claims on the members. The virtues themselves should
be State-organized or made compulsory because this is the only
effective way of exercising them in the cases in question. These
arguments are all relevant to another case considered below,
100 that of education.

A *In the following précis of the first paragraph, fill in the blanks with
the correct word chosen from each group*

Before the State intervened, health was the individual's — 27
[responsibility/duty/concern/function]. He had to — 44 [hope/
look/pay/search] for medical treatment or he might receive it
from some philanthropic society. Out of this system two — 10

3

[advantages/disappointments/abuses/corollaries] emerged; the
poor were — **60** [bullied/neglected/maltreated/diseased] and the
rich were — **37** [ignored/misled/exploited/pampered]. — **71**
[Impartial/Widespread/Intense/Biased] benevolence and, in the
doctors, a higher degree of — **18** [skill/altruism/honesty/co-
operation] would have — **64** [cancelled/intensified/rectified/
alleviated] these abuses.

B *Choose the best alternative*
39 *'Cash nexus' (line 14) means*
    (*a*) the system by which people earn and spend money
          amongst themselves
    (*b*) the desire for money
    (*c*) the system of taxation
    (*d*) the cost of living

 2 *The State had to take action concerning public health because*
    (*a*) poor people could not afford to pay a doctor
    (*b*) no one can protect himself against epidemics
    (*c*) philanthropic societies could no longer afford their work
    (*d*) doctors exploited their patients
    (*e*) no one was forced to seek medical treatment

52 *Political theory can do no more than*
    (*a*) prove the necessity for State control
    (*b*) indicate three methods of controlling public health
    (*c*) work out the proportions of the three methods
    (*d*) ensure that public amenities are kept clean
    (*e*) demand State doctors

C
34 *Which word in the sentence beginning 'This might have justified . . .' (line 11) did the writer italicize in his book?*

58 *Which single word in paragraph 2 refers back to the phrase in
paragraph 1 (line 16) 'unnecessary operations'?*

D *Précis the last three paragraphs in not more than 250 words.*

E 'These arguments are all relevant to another case . . .
that of education' *(line 98). What features of education in this
country in general terms might correspond to*

22 payment for medical treatment

4

68 the voluntary societies

30 the germ theory

5 the distinction between positive health and freedom from disease?

F *Argue, in not more than a hundred words, the theory behind State control of education, following the stages of J. D. Mabbott's argument on health as closely as you can.*

Here is a paragraph from Shaw's preface to The Doctor's Dilemma. *The date of the preface is 1911.*

It is not the fault of our doctors that the medical service of the community, as at present provided for, is a murderous absurdity. That any sane nation, having observed that you could provide for the supply of bread by giving bakers a pecuniary interest in baking for you, should go on to give a surgeon a pecuniary interest in cutting off your leg, is enough to make one despair of political humanity. But that is precisely what we have done. And the more appalling the mutilation, the more the mutilator is paid. He who corrects the ingrowing toe-nail receives a few shillings: he who cuts your inside out receives hundreds of guineas, except when he does it to a poor person for practice.

G *How many emotive words or phrases can you find in this passage? Specify their implications.*

H *Compare it with the equivalent passage of J. D. Mabbott. Are the meaning and emotional attitude the same?*
Here is a second paragraph from Shaw's preface.

The smattering of science that all – even doctors – pick up from the ordinary newspapers nowadays only makes the doctor more dangerous than he used to be. Wise men used to take care to consult doctors qualified before 1860, who were usually contemptuous of or indifferent to the germ theory and bacteriological therapeutics; but now that these veterans have mostly retired or died, we are left in the hands of the generations which, having heard of miracles much as St Thomas Aquinas heard of angels, suddenly concluded that the whole art of healing could be summed up in the formula: Find the microbe and kill it. And even that they did not know how to do. The simplest way to kill most microbes is to throw them into an open street or river and let the sun shine on them, which explains the fact that when great cities have recklessly thrown all their sewage into the open river the water has sometimes been cleaner twenty miles below the city than thirty miles above it. But doctors instinctively avoid all facts that are reassuring, and eagerly swallow those that make it a marvel that anyone could possibly survive three days in an atmosphere consisting mainly of countless pathogenic germs. They conceive microbes as immortal until slain by a germicide administered by a duly qualified medical man. All through Europe people are adjured, by public notices and even under legal penalties, not to throw their microbes into the sunshine, but to collect them carefully in a handkerchief; shield the handkerchief from the sun in the darkness and warmth of the pocket; and send it to a laundry to be mixed up with everybody else's handkerchiefs, with results only too familiar to local health authorities.

I *Compare Shaw's attitude to the germ theory with Mabbott's.*

J *Imagine yourself a doctor and compose a reply to this paragraph in Shaw's own style.*

K *For discussion*

1. Should the State force me to act benevolently to my neighbour?
2. What right have I to interfere with my neighbour for his good?
3. Does State control necessarily make for greater efficiency?

6

2 Mass Entertainment

† *The Uses of Literacy*, by Richard Hoggart, 1957

I suggested earlier that it would be a mistake to regard the cultural struggle now going on as a straight fight between, say, what *The Times* and the picture-dailies respectively represent. To wish that a majority of the population will ever read *The Times* is to wish that human beings were constitutionally different, and is to fall into an intellectual snobbery. The ability to read the decent weeklies is not a *sine qua non* of the good life. It seems unlikely at any time, and is certainly not likely in any period which those of us now alive are likely to know, that a
10 majority in any class will have strongly intellectual pursuits. There are other ways of being in the truth. The strongest objection to the more trivial popular entertainments is not that they prevent their readers from becoming highbrow, but that they make it harder for people without an intellectual bent to become wise in their own way.

The fact that changes in English society over the last fifty years have greatly increased the opportunities for further education available to the few people who will seek it has, therefore, little direct compensatory bearing on the fact that concurrent
20 changes are bringing about an increased trivialization in productions for the majority. Most readers of a popular modern newspaper/magazine are unlikely ever to read a 'quality' paper, but they used to read an old-style weekly which was in some respects better than their newspaper/magazine. The new-style popular publications fail not because they are poor

7

substitutes for *The Times* but because they are only bloodless imitations of what they purport to be, because they are pallid but slicked-up extensions even of nineteenth-century sensationalism, and a considerable decline from the sinewy sensationalism of Elizabethan vernacular writers. They can be accused (as can all else for which they stand as examples: the thin bonhomie of many television programmes, the popular film, much in commercial radio), not of failing to be highbrow, but of not being truly concrete and personal. The quality of life, the kind of response, the rootedness in a wisdom and maturity which a popular and non-highbrow art can possess may be as valuable in their own ways as those of a highbrow art. These productions do not contribute to a sounder popular art but discourage it. They make their audience less likely to arrive at a wisdom derived from an inner, felt discrimination in their sense of people and their attitude to experience. It is easier to kill the old roots than to replace them with anything comparable. Popular publicists always tell their audience that they need not be ashamed of not being highbrow, that they have their own kinds of maturity. This is true, but it becomes false the moment such people say it, because of the way they say it; that is, because their manner of approach seriously distorts the assumption.

Every tendency I have analysed in popular publications is to be found in some forms of broadcasting – especially in those with commercial connexions – and in some ways more strikingly than in publications. There is the appeal to old decencies, as in programmes with titles like, 'For Your Feeling Heart'; there are the new emphases, the stress on the acquisitive and the novel – 'For Your Feeling Heart – in this programme You may Make Your Pile'. There is the high-powered modern combination of these two, in programmes where intimate personal problems are exposed before an immense audience and the person afflicted 'wins' some money for his participation. There is the lowbrow-gang-spirit of some gramophone-record features in which young men, accompanying their items with a stream of pally patter, offer programmes whose whole composition assumes that whatever the greatest number like most is best and the rest are the aberrations of 'eggheads'. Always the apologists for these programmes make the usual defence – that they are

8

'in good taste – homely – full of the pathos and joy of ordinary lives'; and that they are also 'new – arresting – startling – sensational – full of gusto and handsomely endowed with prizes'.

70   Most mass-entertainments are in the end what D. H. Lawrence described as 'anti-life'. They are full of a corrupt brightness, of improper appeals and moral evasions. To recall instances: they tend towards a view of the world in which progress is conceived as a seeking of material possessions, equality as a moral levelling, and freedom as the ground for endless irresponsible pleasure. These productions belong to a vicarious, spectators' world; they offer nothing which can really grip the brain or heart. They assist a gradual drying-up of the more positive, the fuller, the more co-operative kinds of enjoyment, in

80   which one gains much by giving much. They have intolerable pretensions; and pander to the wish to have things both ways, to do as we want and accept no consequences. A handful of such productions reaches daily the great majority of the population: their effect is both widespread and uniform.

A *Choose the best alternative*

45 *A point made in paragraph* 1 *is that*

(a) the triviality of the picture-dailies matters little

(b) reading decent weeklies is an obstacle to 'the good life'

(c) there are many types of reading that lie between the extremes represented by *The Times* and by the picture-dailies

(d) reading *The Times* is intellectual snobbery

(e) the weakness of the picture-dailies does not lie in their lack of intellectual content

13 *A point made in paragraph* 2 *is that*

(a) better education will make men increasingly impatient of what is trivial

(b) the old-style weekly was more highbrow than the modern newspaper/magazine

(c) prose writing went into a decline because the Elizabethans were so fond of sensationalism

9

(*d*) it is possible to learn much about human relationships without being learned

(*e*) popular publicists do well to assure people that they need not be ashamed of being highbrow

B *Here is a précis of paragraph* 3. *Choose the best of the alternatives in brackets to fill each numbered gap.*

In the same way, some broadcast programmes appeal both to — **38** [decency/compassion/heartiness/loyalty] and to — **19** [greed/jealousy/stress/sense of equality]; while money is — **59** [won/earned/given away/shared], the audience hears of a — **1** [private/serious/common/high-powered] problem. Disc-jockeys imply that — **16** [friendliness/popular taste/good fellowship/composition] is the sole — **65** [arbitration/innuendo/aberration/criterion] of excellence. Such programmes are — **28** [excused/justified/apologized for/loved] on the grounds that they are — **76** [topical/pathetic/not esoteric/tasty] and are also — **8** [lively/astonishing/enjoyable/vivid].

C *Write your own précis of paragraph* 4 *in about fifty words.*

D *Using the general points made by Hoggart, write an essay on* Good and Bad Advertising.

E *Write the memorandum which Hoggart would send to his staff, if he edited a popular paper, on* How to Make this Paper Popular but Not Trivial.

F 'The real division of cultures is not between arts and science but between academic and popular.' *Discuss.*

G *Write an essay on* Sentimentality *or* Materialism.

H (*Research.*) *Find, in the newspapers, some articles of which Hoggart would approve and others of which he would disapprove.*

3 African Independence

† An article by Roland Oliver in *The Listener*, 7 February 1963

The process of decolonization has taught us that there are at least three stages, or levels, of independence. The most obvious and the most easily recognizable stage is political independence. One flag is lowered, another raised in its place. Then there is economic independence, far more subtle and difficult to define. It may coincide, roughly, with political independence, or it may not. Lastly, there is intellectual independence, the subtlest and least measurable stage of all.

10   Many Europeans and Africans imagine that intellectual independence was something that had been achieved, at least by some elements of the former colonial peoples, long before political independence, by the opportunity of sharing, through education, in the cultural heritage of Western civilization. An educated African, it was imagined, was intellectually, at least, a liberated African. He had mastered the civilization of his colonizers. He had become a citizen of the world. The last thing that an intellectually liberated African was thought to require was any knowledge of Africa. He had turned his back on all that. The study of African languages, religion, anthro-
20 pology, archaeology, history, music, and art – all these were felt to be the concern only of a few specialists, scattered over the world at large. They were not thought to be connected with the progress of Africans towards intellectual liberation. And in retrospect nothing is more striking than the suspicion with

11

which most Africans regarded African studies, until the attainment of political independence was well in sight. So long as the colonial period lasted, African studies were regarded, especially by the educated Africans, as retrogressive, as an attempt to put the clock back and to palm them off with something second-rate.

30 This, far more than any intellectual or imaginative rigidity of European educators in Africa, was the real bar to the adaptation of cultural subjects in African schools and universities towards the African environment to which they had been transplanted.

Yet no sooner was political independence achieved in West Africa, and no sooner was it well in sight in the rest of tropical Africa, than there arose a sudden and widespread demand for a corresponding emancipation in the fields of religion and culture. The total westernization, which had been so uncompromisingly fought for before political independence, now ceased to be the

40 ideal. The political separation from the colonial powers suddenly brought to light a sense of cultural nakedness which had to be covered, a lack of identity which had to be made good. So, as the struggle for political independence reached its final climax, Africans started to wear so-called national dress, and to rename their countries or their political parties after such symbols as they could find of a glorious pre-colonial past – Ghana, Mali, the Zimbabwe African Peoples' Union. Traditional cults, long dormant or at least deeply concealed, re-emerged into the light of day.

50 At a less popular level, in schools and universities, a demand arose, strongly backed by the new national governments, for the academic pursuit of African studies – for a re-examination of African history, religious ideas, legal principles, social institutions, drama and music, in which the lead should be taken by Africans in the interpretation of things African, both internally and to the outside world. During the last few years the African universities, or some of them, have responded to this demand by achieving a modest adaptation of their courses to the African environment. But this has been largely on the initiative of

60 individual teachers, unsupported for the most part by competent research institutions – except perhaps in the field of social anthropology, which is, significantly, the one branch of African studies about which Africans remain deeply suspicious. Anthropology apart, it is still the case that the most

powerful research centres in African studies are to be found in
countries outside Africa; London, Paris, Moscow, Brussels, Los
Angeles – all these have many more scholars working in African
subjects than any university in Africa itself.

A *Choose the best alternative*
23 *The writer adds* 'or levels' *(line 2) because*
  (a) the three types of independence are not necessarily in
      succession
  (b) 'level' can mean the same as 'stage'
  (c) the word 'stage' can mean so many things
  (d) the word 'levels' shows that the writer has social dis-
      tinctions in mind
  (e) he is looking ahead to the phrase, 'One flag is lowered'

43 'Subtle' *(line 7) means*
  (a) cunning (b) hair-splitting (c) undermining (d) intangible
  (e) remote

73 *Paragraph 2*
  (a) shows how hard intellectual independence is to measure
  (b) equates intellectual independence with western educa-
      tion
  (c) shows how intellectual independence was once mis-
      interpreted
  (d) is primarily an attack on education in Africa
  (e) clears away a misconception in the reader's mind about
      intellectual independence

21 'They' *(line 33) must refer to*
  (a) European educators in Africa
  (b) Cultural subjects
  (c) African schools and universities
  (d) The Africans
  (e) African studies

57 'Corresponding' *(line 37) looks back to*
  (a) widespread (b) tropical (c) political (d) independence
  (e) West Africa

 6 *African culture had not figured in academic curricula because*
  (a) the imperial powers discouraged it

(b) the administration was narrow-minded

(c) it could not be taught

(d) it was not thought useful

(e) the Africans wanted to free themselves from the past

63 *By a* 'lack of identity' *(line 42) the writer means that Africans*

(a) had no ideals with which to associate themselves

(b) took no interest in their own history

(c) felt they had inherited no distinctive character

(d) could think of no other nations like themselves

(e) suddenly missed the administrative help given by Europe

26 *By the word* 'modest' *(line 58) the writer implies that the universities*

(a) have shown themselves humble

(b) have quietly adopted new courses

(c) have not radically altered their courses

(d) have eliminated anything shocking from their courses

(e) have not made extravagant claims for their courses

51 *By* 'significantly' *(line 62) the writer means that Africans' suspicion of anthropology reveals their*

(a) self-consciousness about their primitive past

(b) distrust of change

(c) lack of interest in academic subjects

(d) dislike of Western cultures

(e) energy for the future

35 *The writer implies that African universities, in developing African studies, have been for the most part*

(a) co-operative (b) obstructive (c) incompetent (d) dilatory (e) progressive

11 *Support your answer to 35 by quoting words or phrases that convey the implication.*

54 *Write down the three words (not proper names) used in this extract, which have most recently joined the English language. What comment have you on their formation?*

B *For discussion*

Might the three levels of independence apply to adolescents when they first leave their homes and earn their own living?

What equivalent to the three 'levels' do you see? In particular, consider the equivalent of intellectual independence (What forms does it take? Why do young people want it? How do they seek to attain it?).

C *Do you feel a need for your own country to have a 'cultural identity'? Write about some of its cultural traditions; consider how widespread they really are and work out their values and shortcomings.*

4 The Eighteenth Century

† *English Social History*, by G. M. Trevelyan, 1946

The first forty years of the Eighteenth Century, the reign of Anne and the rule of Walpole, constitute an age of transition, during which the feuds and ideals of the Stuart era, lately a lava flood scouring the land with devastating heat, were being chan-nelled and congealed into fixed, durable Hanoverian forms. In this way the age of Marlborough and Bolingbroke, of Swift and Defoe, was the meeting point of two epochs. It is only in the years that followed (1740–1780) that we find a generation of men wholly characteristic of the Eighteenth Century ethos, a society
10 with a mental outlook of its own, self-poised, self-judged, and self-approved, freed from the disturbing passions of the past, and not yet troubled with anxieties about a very different future which was soon to be brought upon the scene by the Industrial and the French Revolutions. The gods mercifully gave mankind this little moment of peace between the religious fanaticisms of the past and the fanaticisms of class and race that were speedily to arise and dominate time to come. In England it was an age of aristocracy and liberty; of the rule of law and the absence of reform; of individual initiative and institutional
20 decay; of Latitudinarianism above and Wesleyanism below; of the growth of humanitarian and philanthropic feeling and endeavour; of creative vigour in all the trades and arts that serve and adorn the life of man.

It is a 'classical age', that is to say an age of unchallenged assumptions, when the philosophers of the street, such as Dr Johnson, have ample leisure to moralize on the human scene, in the happy belief that the state of society and the modes of

thought to which they are accustomed are not mere passing aspects of an ever-shifting kaleidoscope, but permanent habita-
30 tions, the final outcome of reason and experience. Such an age does not aspire to progress though it may in fact be progressing; it regards itself not as setting out but as having arrived; it is thankful for what it has, and enjoys life without 'deep questioning which probes to endless dole'. And therefore the men of this 'classical' age looked back with a sense of kinship to the far-off Ancient World. The upper class regarded the Greeks and Romans as honorary Englishmen, their precursors in liberty and culture, and the Roman Senate as the prototype of the British Parliament. The mediaeval period, with its 'gothic' aspirations
40 and barbarisms, sank for a while below the horizon of study and sympathy, so that the eye of taste could range back without hindrance across the gulf of time, and contemplate on its further shore the only civilization which could claim to be as classical, as poised, as enlightened and as artistic as the fortunate present.

Compared to the self-complacency of the mid-Eighteenth Century, the proverbial self-complacency of the Victorians is modesty itself, for the Victorians were, within certain limits, ardent and successful reformers, and admired themselves for
50 the improvements they made. But to the typical men of the period of Blackstone, Gibbon and Burke, England appeared to be the best country possible in an imperfect world, requiring only to be left alone where Providence and the revolution of 1688 had so fortunately placed her. Their optimism about England was based on a general pessimism about the human race, not on a belief in perpetual and world-wide 'progress' such as cheered simple hearts in the Nineteenth Century.

It is true that the men who were least content were those who looked closest at the realities of English life – Hogarth, Fielding,
60 Smollett and the philanthropists; they indeed exposed particular evils as unsparingly as Dickens himself. But even their strictures kept within the limits of the classical and conservative philosophy of the time. Nor was the self-complacency of that age altogether unjustified, though it was unfortunate because it sustained an atmosphere inimical to any general movement of reform. It was a society which, with all its grave faults, was brilliant above and stable below.

17

A *Paragraph 1. In which of the four periods (a) before 1700, (b) 1700–1740, (c) 1740–1780, (d) after 1780, is the writer placing each of the following?*

56 transition; **15** lava flood; **36** fixed durable forms; **74** congealment; **25** meeting point; **61** Swift; **31** eighteenth-century ethos; **46** religious passions; **9** class fanaticisms; **53** institutional decay; **40** Stuart era; **4** Wesleyanism; **55** moment of peace; **29** Industrial Revolution.

B *Paragraph 2. Choose the best alternative*

77 *Dr Johnson is called a philosopher of the street (line 25) because*

    (*a*) he was an absolutely ordinary person
    (*b*) he was an immoral person
    (*c*) he spoke out-of-doors
    (*d*) he was a talker but not a writer
    (*e*) he generalized about everyday matters.

49 'To moralize on the human scene' (*line 26*) *means*

    (*a*) to discuss how people behave
    (*b*) to discuss how people used to behave
    (*c*) to discuss how people ought to behave
    (*d*) to give instructions about how people are to behave
    (*e*) to improve the morale of the people.

20 'Which probes to endless dole' (*line 34*) *means*

    (*a*) which hurts by its insistent searching
    (*b*) which never stops asking
    (*c*) which reaches the limits of speculation
    (*d*) which enquires about unemployment
    (*e*) which criticizes every answer.

66 'Therefore' (*line 34*) *implies that the Ancient World*

    (*a*) was self-satisfied
    (*b*) established a firm society
    (*c*) showed the eighteenth century what being 'classical' meant
    (*d*) did not question deeply
    (*e*) had ample leisure.

72 'honorary Englishmen' (*line 37*) *means*

    (*a*) decent Englishmen (*b*) unpaid Englishmen (*c*) early Englishmen (*d*) Englishmen in spirit (*e*) almost Englishmen.

33 'Gothic' (*line 39*) *is placed in inverted commas because*

    (*a*) it is an architectural term

    (*b*) it is slang

    (*c*) it refers directly to the Goths

    (*d*) it was originally a term of abuse

    (*e*) it is a foreign word

70 'without hindrance' (*line 41*) *means*

    (*a*) with nothing else intervening

    (*b*) with no demand for deep study

    (*c*) with no modern preconceptions

    (*d*) with no backward looks

    (*e*) with many backward looks

C *Paragraphs 1 and 2. There are three sections of elaborate metaphor here.*

48 *In which of these does the author make little attempt at sustaining the metaphor – that is to say, at making a number of words fit the same picture?*

7 *In which does he sustain the metaphor with success?*

41 *In which does he make an attempt to sustain the metaphor, but confuse it with one inappropriate word?*

D *Paragraphs 3 and 4. For each statement below, put a √ if it is stated or implied in these two paragraphs, a × if it is denied (directly or indirectly) in these two paragraphs, or a ? if these two paragraphs give us no evidence either way.*

24 The complacency of the eighteenth century was inevitable.

75 The complacency of the eighteenth century exceeded that of the nineteenth century.

50 The men of the eighteenth century were complacent only about their own country.

12 Complacency was the enemy of reform in the eighteenth century.

69 Complacency in the eighteenth century was linked with a belief in progress.

32 The men of the eighteenth century were glad that there had been a revolution in 1688.

62 The simple hearts of the eighteenth century were not easily cheered.

17 The philanthropists made an outright attack on eighteenth-century complacency.

42 A close look at eighteenth-century realities tended to weaken complacency.

3 The eighteenth century paid no attention to Dickens.

47 There were some grounds for complacency in the eighteenth century.

67 The lower classes were seething with discontent in the eighteenth century.

14 *Which of the above statements is nonsense? Why?*

E *Discuss the writer's tone in this piece. Do you find irony? admiration? envy? scorn? a suggestion that the eighteenth century has been misunderstood? a desire to give both sides of the picture? Illustrate what you write by quoting particular words and phrases (or giving the numbers of the lines concerned).*

F *Write an essay on* Self-satisfaction.

G *(Research.) What evidence can you find, outside this passage, for and against the view that the eighteenth century was a complacent age?*

5 Convention

† *Man, Morals and Society*, by J. C. Flugel, 1955

[*The blank numbered spaces in this extract may be completed from the list of words in exercise* **B**, *p. 24.*]

Convention would seem to possess two main real advantages, one primarily individual, the other social. The first lies in the fact that, in prescribing within narrow limits what has to be done, said, or worn, it saves us from the mental effort of thinking or deciding for ourselves and provides us, so to speak, with a number of formulae (which may, as Pear suggests, have value as social lubricants) for use on suitable occasions. In this it is like habit, but of course it shares with habit the disadvantage that it may lead us to behave in ways that, with changing cir-
10 cumstances, may have ceased to be appropriate. The second, social, advantage of convention consists in helping to preserve the solidarity of the groups or classes concerned. Our judgement as to its value in this last respect will largely depend upon how far we consider the retention of such groups and classes is desirable. Those who demand a classless society will rightly look upon many of our conventions with a certain suspicion.

In any case, however, conventions imply rules and — **4** (we can indeed without serious inaccuracy call them taboos) which are usually — **11** and often in themselves absurd. The frequently
20 pilloried convention of New York men to change from one kind of hat to another on a certain date, regardless of the weather, falls into this category. It is likewise not easy to find a satisfactory reason why men should be expected to remove their hats on entering a house (as distinct from a shop – in this country at least) while women are supposed to await an invitation from their hostess before doing so; though the origin of this — **36** may have something to do with a religious differentiation between the implications of men's and women's headgear.

The taboo in this country on dickies, loose cuffs, and made-up
30 ties could perhaps be — 62 as an objection to an element of
pretence and spuriousness (since cuffs and dickies suggest that
they are — 23 parts of a shirt, and ties suggest that they have
actually been tied for the occasion), but this does not hold of
waistcoats, which, though highly respectable, reveal themselves
if the coat be removed, as no less — 68 behind than a dicky
is in front. The speed with which fashions in clothes can change
and the ease with which we adapt ourselves to them (even, to
take an extreme example, to doing without clothes altogether,
as in a nudist camp) would seem to show that particular con-
40 ventions and taboos of this sort do not depend to any large
extent on any — 41 factor of usefulness, beauty, or convenience,
or even on any deeper symbolic significance, but that social
approval and desire for — 8 are the chief influences at work.
Nevertheless there can be no doubt about the very real feelings
of guilty — 49 that failure to conform can produce in most
people – and these feelings are very similar to those aroused
by the — 33 of more primitive and permanent taboos.

Little need be said about good manners; indeed, as already
indicated, the boundary between them and conventions is
50 difficult to draw. Perhaps the chief difference is that manners
apply to relatively intimate and personal contacts and relationships. It would be a breach of convention to appear in bathing
costume in a city street, but a breach of manners to attend a
private party thus attired. Good manners, moreover, to a higher
degree than conventions and superstitions, often have a sound
rational and ethical basis, inasmuch as they may save our
fellows from reasonably grounded inconvenience, discomfort,
and embarrassment. It is good manners, for instance, to refrain
from talking or quoting a foreign language which some of those
60 listening would not understand; in fact, quite generally, good
manners imply behaviour that puts people at their ease. The
trouble with manners is that they often tend to outlive their
usefulness and to degenerate into mere conventions. It is usually
thought that the custom of allowing a woman to walk on the
inside of the pavement dates from the period when the contents
of household utensils were thrown from upper windows into
the central gutter of the street with no more ceremony than a
warning cry, and that the gentleman by taking the outer

22

position gallantly exposed himself in greater degree to the danger
70 that threatened from above. But in modern towns slops are not
emptied through the windows, and the convention may involve
an amount of unnecessary dodging and shifting of a kind that
to a psychiatrist unconversant with the practice might easily
suggest that the gentleman was suffering from a phobia or an
obsession.

A *In paragraph 1*

In analysing the effects of convention, the writer — **71** [contradicts/
qualifies/supports/justifies/refutes] *his recognition of its con-
veniences by indicating that it may easily —* **15** [fossilize/decay/
demoralize us/die out/change].

61 *An example of the* 'formulae' *(line 6) might be*

    (*a*) the area of a circle is πr^2
    (*b*) 'How do you do?'
    (*c*) driving, in the United Kingdom, on the left-hand side of
    the road
    (*d*) stamping envelopes on the top right-hand corner
    (*e*) reading a newspaper at breakfast.

42 'Appropriate' *(line 10) to what?*

    (*a*) modern times (*b*) the past (*c*) social occasions (*d*) our
    wishes (*e*) others' wishes.

26 *The writer's outlook, to judge from paragraph 1, is*

    (*a*) very conservative (*b*) on the whole conservative (*c*)
    neutral (*d*) on the whole radical (*e*) extremely radical.

65 *A convention that would illustrate the second part of paragraph
1 is*

    (*a*) shaking hands (*b*) bank holidays (*c*) tipping a waiter
    (*d*) helping an old lady across the road (*e*) changing for
    dinner

45 *Which of these statements is not reflected in paragraph 1?*

    (*a*) habit makes us old-fashioned
    (*b*) conventions keep class barriers erected
    (*c*) conventions strengthen existing communities
    (*d*) conventions often make us act without dignity
    (*e*) conventions can help a man form acquaintances

B *In paragraph 2, pick out the word actually used by the writer for each numbered gap.*

4 discipline/restrictions/permits/bureaucracy

11 arbitrary/laughable/pointless/well thought-out

36 paradox/routine/discrimination/distinction

62 qualified/rationalized/dismissed/reckoned

23 removable/indispensable/integral/actual

68 disreputable/unsafe/efficient/spurious

41 intrinsic/particular/compelling/other

8 individuality/unanimity/prosperity/conformity

49 misery/wrong-doing/discomfort/punishment

33 worship/erection/destruction/infringement

C

74 *Summarize paragraph 3 in not more than 70 words. There is no need to mention any of the examples.*

D *Distinguish, with examples*
  1. convention, habit, custom, etiquette, ritual
  2. unconventional, eccentric, abnormal, unusual, rare, strange

E *Rewrite paragraph 1, including all the points made, as if you were*
  1. very conservative 2. sweepingly egalitarian

F *Give examples of the writer's humour and caution. What impression do you form of his style?*

G *How would you judge that someone was*
  1. conservative (*not* Conservative) 2. well-mannered
  3. a hypocrite?

H *Comment on the following passages in the light of J. C. Flugel's three paragraphs.*

(*a*) He quite took to Mrs Walshingham. He was impressed by her conspicuous tact and refinement; it seemed to him that the ladylike could go no farther. She was always dressed with a delicate fussiness that was never disarranged, and even a sort of faded quality about her hair, and face, and bearing, and emotions, contributed to her effect. Kipps was not a big man, and

commonly he did not feel a big man, but with Mrs Walshingham he always felt enormous and distended, as though he was
a navvy who had taken some disagreeable poison which puffed
him up inside his skin as a preliminary to bursting. He felt, too,
as though he had been rolled in clay and his hair dressed with
gum. And he felt that his voice was strident and his accent
like somebody swinging a crowded pig's-tail in a free and care-
less manner. All this increased and enforced his respect for her.
Her hand, which flitted often and again to his hand and arm,
was singularly shaped and cool. 'Arthur', she called him from
the very beginning.

She did not so much positively teach and tell him as tact-
fully guide and infect him. Her conversation was not so much
didactic as exemplary. She would say, '*I do* like people to do' so
and so. She would tell him anecdotes of nice things done, of
gentlemanly feats of graceful consideration; she would record
her neat observations of people in trains and omnibuses, how,
for example, a man had passed her change to the conductor,
'quite a common man he looked', but he had lifted his hat. She
stamped Kipps so deeply with the hat-raising habit that he
would uncover if he found himself in the same railway ticket-
office with a lady, and so stand ceremoniously until the difficulties of change drove him to an apologetic provisional oblique
resumption of his headgear. . . .

(H. G. Wells, Kipps, 1905)

(*b*) When the ladies returned to the drawing-room, there was
little to be done but to hear Lady Catherine talk, which she did
without any intermission till coffee came in, delivering her
opinion on every subject in so decisive a manner as proved she
was not used to have her judgment controverted. She inquired
into Charlotte's domestic concerns familiarly and minutely,
and gave her a great deal of advice as to the management of
them all; told her how everything ought to be regulated in so
small a family as hers, and instructed her as to the care of her
cows and her poultry. Elizabeth found that nothing was beneath
this great lady's attention which could furnish her with an
occasion for dictating to others. In the intervals of her dis-
course with Mrs. Collins, she addressed a variety of questions
to Maria and Elizabeth, but especially to the latter, of whose

connexions she knew the least, and who, she observed to Mrs Collins, was a very genteel, pretty kind of girl. She asked her at different times how many sisters she had, whether they were older or younger than herself, whether any of them were likely to be married, whether they were handsome, where they had been educated, what carriage her father kept, and what had been her mother's maiden name? Elizabeth felt all the impertinence of her questions, but answered them very composedly.

(Jane Austen, *Pride and Prejudice*, 1813)

(c) Having mentioned laughing, I must particularly warn you against it: and I could heartily wish that you may often be seen to smile, but never heard to laugh while you live. Frequent and loud laughter is the characteristic of folly and ill manners: it is the manner in which the mob express their silly joy at silly things; and they call it being merry. In my mind there is nothing so illiberal and so ill-bred, as audible laughter. . . . I am neither of a melancholy, nor a cynical disposition, and am as willing, and as apt, to be pleased as anybody; but I am sure that, since I had the full use of reason, nobody has ever heard me laugh.

(Lord Chesterfield, letter to his son. 9 March 1748)

6 Insurance

Article by Katharine Whitehorn in *The Spectator*,
19 October 1962

I used to think that the best way of annoying an insurance man
was to point out that when he insures your jewellery against
theft he is simply betting you it won't be stolen. You can bet
him it will rain on the day of the church fête, bet him you'll die
before you are fifty; you can bet him your motor-car will be
unable to resist the temptation to run into other motor-cars;
and he, with amazing optimism, will bet you it won't; and if he
is wrong, he pays up. But I have since found that you can make
insurance people just as angry by suggesting it is high time they
10 came under some form of government control.

Mind you, I know plenty of people who wouldn't be where
they are but for insurance, and I do not just mean important
men from the Pru in hospital suffering from cracked skulls.
There is the young couple who have decorated their house on
the proceeds of a fire started by a tramp in the attic, a tramp
now being sought eagerly by all their friends; and one of the
nicest skirts my mother ever had replaced one on which she had
leaned too long and too meditatively at the ironing-board.
There are even subtler ways of playing the insurance game: I
20 know of a man (I had better not be too precise about this)
whose fowls mysteriously develop pest in exact relation to his
overdraft, since the Government insures you against this by
compensating you for their compulsory destruction; it is quite
as good a racket as the old-fashioned fire in a flagging fur firm.

But few have the chance actually to profit from insurance. All
that most people want is a protection from disaster – and a
chance to know to which disasters the protection applies.

('Come back!' shouted Elizabeth Beresford once to a man who was photographing a snake, 'You're not insured for that!')
30 And it is presumably up to us whether we succeed in guessing correctly what disasters we may encounter. Skaters insure their legs and singers their voices; I suppose there is no reason why politicians should not insure their smiles, and dons could even insure their brains, except that it would be so hard to substantiate a claim. Personally, I would like most to insure against loss of insurance certificates and loss of temper. But in such cases, it is plainly up to us how, what and whether we insure.

Not so with car insurance: it is exacted by law; so that the whims of insurance companies can often take on the force of
40 law. It is well known that certain companies refuse altogether to insure certain categories of people, like students and actors; and no doubt, statistically, they have a perfectly sound case. It seems to be less widely known how readily a company will refuse insurance to a car on which it has already had to pay up twice, regardless of *why* it had to pay – I heard of a girl, for example, whose first smash was just one of those things, but whose second was caused by leaving her car under a tree which subsequently fell down. Plenty of people do not put in claims when they could because they are so afraid of the company
50 refusing to insure them next time, and once one company has refused you it may be almost impossible to get another one to take you on.

Now I know that there are people who, though it is never their own fault, are accident-prone in a statistically recognisable sense. It is always *their* aeroplanes which are fog-bound, *their* heads that are underneath the falling brick, *their* darkened halls in which people leave unsuspected prams: look at all those people who are always the one to find the bluebottle in the lettuce. And so the insurance companies say, understandably,
60 that they are less interested in whose fault these things are than in staying clear of such people altogether. And if commerce was all that was involved, it would be fair enough. But where you get insurance insisted upon by law, as in the case of third-party risk, then it is not fair enough: because law must not be right in general but unjust in particular cases. Statistically, it might pay to imprison every teenager with an ugly smile, or slap a poll tax on every successful businessman, on the grounds that the

one will probably end up by thieving and the other is almost certainly fiddling his income tax. But however statistically satis-
70 fying it might be it would still be judicially revolting because in law you have to prove that it is the individual, and not the type, that is at fault.

By their power to refuse insurance the companies at the moment also have the power to keep people off the roads, even if these people have committed no offence in law. It seems to me that the Government is putting a good deal of business in the companies' way by demanding compulsory third-party insurance, and that it would be perfectly reasonable for it to require in return that they standardise premiums and accept
80 everyone legally permitted to drive. People who get licences to run ferries, after all, have to take the roughs with the smoothies even if the former are likely to be sick over the floor; and they have to keep up the services at uneconomic times of day as well as rush hours. So long as insurance is required by law, it ought to be required by law to behave fairly.

And while they are about it, they could clean up this business about the supposed value of the object insured in other fields. Insure your stamp album for five hundred pounds; lose it; discover that its market value is in fact four hundred, and four
90 hundred is what you get. Find that it is worth six hundred and you will still not get a penny over five. I know this is determined by the ruling that you can only insure a genuine loss to your-self – I cannot, for example, insure the life of General de Gaulle and sit back hoping the next assassination will succeed. But it would surely be possible to establish that the loss must genuinely affect the person, without making that the measure of the extent of the loss? It is logical to insure a given sum for a given premium: a straight bet for a straight sum. It is equally logical to insure for replacement value, whatever that may happen to
100 be. But to make it replacement value or the sum insured, whichever happens to be the smaller, is heads you lose, tails we don't pay up.

I cannot help feeling, too, that we could do with a firmer mechanism for making insurance companies pay up promptly. Insurance companies tell you that promptness in settling up is one of the things which distinguish the big/expensive/reputable companies from the little tin-pot places; but I have never heard of any company, however tin-pot, that accepted an interminable delay in our side of the bargain – the premiums. I would have thought it possible to make insurance companies liable to pay within a fixed short time unless they lodged with the courts a doubt as to the fairness of the claim; and, side by side with that, a penalty imposed on any company which lodged such a claim if the court then decided it had no good reason for lodging it.

Obviously, these various reforms might result in slightly higher premiums all round; but I think it would be worth it for the sake of fairness. Insurance exists, after all, to level out the unfairness of life; to be a way of combating the fact that one bloke's brake-block breaks and the next bloke's does not. It is the net under the tightrope; and if the net itself has holes in it, the whole thing becomes pointless; since there is no known way of insuring against the unfairness of an insurance company.

A

　1 *Summarize the argument, representing each paragraph in the original by one sentence in your summary.*

B *Explain clearly in your own words (and without giving examples) the distinction between 'commerce' and 'law' in the fifth paragraph. How is this connected with the distinction between the type and the individual?*

C *What is the equivalent in car insurance of*

56 a licence to run a ferry

16 ferry-passengers likely to be sick over the floor

69 uneconomic times of day?

D *Write an article, similar in style to this one, from the insurance man's point of view.*

E *Comment on the first and last paragraphs of this essay. Do you learn anything useful from them about beginning and ending your own essays? Discuss the difference between academic writing and popular writing, and between journalism and journalese.*

F *Write a letter to Miss Whitehorn, asking her to produce a similar article on 'School Authorities' and furnishing her with useful material.*

7 The State and the Writer

† 'The Prevention of Literature', by George Orwell (in *Selected Essays*), 1945

The organized lying practised by totalitarian states is not, as is sometimes claimed, a temporary expedient of the same nature as military deception. It is something integral to totalitarianism, something that would still continue even if concentration camps and secret police forces had ceased to be necessary. Among intelligent Communists there is an underground legend to the effect that although the Russian government is obliged now to deal in lying propaganda, frame-up trials, and so forth, it is secretly recording the true facts and will publish them at some future time. We can, I believe, be quite certain that this is not the case, because the mentality implied by such an action is that of a liberal historian who believes that the past cannot be altered and that a correct knowledge of history is valuable as a matter of course. From the totalitarian point of view history is something to be created rather than learned. A totalitarian state is in effect a theocracy, and its ruling caste, in order to keep its position, has to be thought of as infallible. But since, in practice, no one is infallible, it is frequently necessary to rearrange past events in order to show that this or that mistake was not made, or that this or that imaginary triumph actually happened. Then, again, every major change in policy demands a corresponding change of doctrine and a revaluation of prominent historical figures. This kind of thing happens everywhere, but is clearly likelier to lead

to outright falsification in societies where only one opinion is permissible at any given moment. Totalitarianism demands, in fact, the continuous alteration of the past, and in the long run probably demands a disbelief in the very existence of objective truth. The friends of totalitarianism in this country
30 usually tend to argue that since absolute truth is not attainable, a big lie is no worse than a little lie. It is pointed out that all historical records are biased and inaccurate, or, on the other hand, that modern physics has proved that what seems to us the real world is an illusion, so that to believe in the evidence of one's senses is simply vulgar philistinism. A totalitarian society which succeeded in perpetuating itself would probably set up a schizophrenic system of thought, in which the laws of common sense held good in everyday life and in certain exact sciences, but could be disregarded by the politician, the his-
40 torian, and the sociologist. Already there are countless people who would think it scandalous to falsify a scientific textbook, but would see nothing wrong in falsifying an historical fact. It is at the point where literature and politics cross that totalitarianism exerts its greatest pressure on the intellectual. The exact sciences are not, at this date, menaced to anything like the same extent. This partly accounts for the fact that in all countries it is easier for the scientists than for the writers to line up behind their respective governments.

To keep the matter in perspective, let me repeat what I said
50 at the beginning of this essay: that in England the *immediate* enemies of truthfulness, and hence of freedom of thought, are the Press lords, the film magnates, and the bureaucrats, but that on a long view the weakening of the desire for liberty among the intellectuals themselves is the most serious symptom of all. It may seem that all this time I have been talking about the effects of censorship, not on literature as a whole, but merely on one department of political journalism. Granted that Soviet Russia constitutes a sort of forbidden area in the British Press, granted that issues like Poland, the Spanish Civil War, the
60 Russo-German pact, and so forth, are debarred from serious discussion, and that if you possess information that conflicts with the prevailing orthodoxy you are expected either to distort it or keep quiet about it – granted all this, why should literature in the wider sense be affected? Is every writer a

politician, and is every book necessarily a work of straight-forward 'reportage'? Even under the tightest dictatorship, cannot the individual writer remain free inside his own mind and distil or disguise his unorthodox ideas in such a way that the authorities will be too stupid to recognize them? And in any
70 case, if the writer himself is in agreement with the prevailing orthodoxy, why should it have a cramping effect on him? Is not literature, or any of the arts, likeliest to flourish in societies in which there are no major conflicts of opinion and no sharp distinction between the artist and his audience? Does one have to assume that every writer is a rebel, or even that a writer as such is an exceptional person?

Whenever one attempts to defend intellectual liberty against the claims of totalitarianism, one meets with these arguments in one form or another. They are based on a complete misunder-
80 standing of what literature is, and how – one should perhaps rather say *why* – it comes into being. They assume that a writer is either a mere entertainer or else a venal hack who can switch from one line of propaganda to another as easily as an organ grinder changing tunes. But, after all, how is it that books ever come to be written? Above a quite low level, literature is an attempt to influence the viewpoint of one's contemporaries by recording experience. And so far as freedom of expression is concerned, there is not much difference between a mere journalist and the most 'unpolitical' imaginative writer. The
90 journalist is unfree, and is conscious of unfreedom, when he is forced to write lies or suppress what seems to him important news: the imaginative writer is unfree when he has to falsify his subjective feelings, which from his point of view are facts. He may distort and caricature reality in order to make his meaning clearer, but he cannot misrepresent the scenery of his own mind: he cannot say with any conviction that he likes what he dislikes, or believes what he disbelieves. If he is forced to do so, the only result is that his creative faculties dry up. Nor can he solve the problem by keeping away from controversial topics.
100 There is no such thing as genuinely non-political literature, and least of all in an age like our own, when fears, hatreds, and loyalties of a directly political kind are near to the surface of everyone's consciousness. Even a single taboo can have an all-round crippling effect upon the mind, because there is always

33

the danger that any thought which is freely followed up may lead to the forbidden thought. It follows that the atmosphere of totalitarianism is deadly to any kind of prose writer, though a poet, at any rate a lyric poet, might possibly find it breathable. And in any totalitarian society that survives for more than a 110 couple of generations, it is probable that prose literature, of the kind that has existed during the past four hundred years, must actually come to an end.

A *George Orwell has been outlining the suppressions and distortions practised by the Russian government and its publicists at the time of his writing (1945). He claims that the lies put out by the Russians had been meekly accepted by left-wing thinkers in Britain and that therefore these lies might well be perpetuated.*

He now (paragraph 1) mentions a defence, heard on some communist lips, of the 'organized lying'. This first defence is, put briefly, that (choose two)

38 (a) the lying is a means to an end
(b) the lying is imposed by intelligent communists only
(c) there is no such thing as historical truth
(d) the lying is carried on with the will of the people
(e) there will soon be no need for the lies

Orwell sees no truth whatsoever in this claim, for, he says, a totalitarian state (choose two)

19 (a) by definition cannot be wrong
(b) depends upon a ruling class
(c) finds it easy to rewrite history
(d) constantly revalues historical figures
(e) must ultimately dictate opinions

Assuming the acceptance of this argument, Orwell goes on to state a second possible defence of communist practice – 'A big lie is no worse than a little lie.' Those making this second defence

29 (a) accept the absence of objective standards
(b) rely wholly on modern physics
(c) recruit the theory of relativity as an ally
(d) point to the comparative security of scientists in totalitarian state
(e) ask us to believe our senses

Orwell starts demolishing this defence at the words

3 (a) 'It is pointed out . . .' (*line 31*)
    (b) 'A totalitarian society . . .' (*line 35*)
    (c) 'Already there are countless folk . . .' (*line 40*)
    (d) 'It is at the point . . .' (*line 42*)
    (e) 'To keep the matter in perspective . . .' (*line 49*)

and does so by (choose two)

58 (a) pointing to an absurd inconsistency (if so what?)
    (b) saying that politicians, historians and sociologists need not accept official beliefs
    (c) pointing out the distress that the individual thinker must eventually undergo
    (d) accepting a distinction between historical and scientific fact
    (e) denying that anyone now believes the evidence of his senses

At the beginning of the second paragraph, Orwell tries to redress a false emphasis that his readers may have accepted, as the phrase 'to keep the matter in perspective' tells us. He is obviously reluctant to give us the impression that (choose two)

12 (a) his last criticism applies at all to England
    (b) he ignores the baneful effects on freedom of speech in England of monopolies and 'official lines'
    (c) intellectuals in England are seriously affected
    (d) intellectuals in England have lost initiative
    (e) the 'double-think' that he has just described is already entrenched in England

He now enlarges the literary range; granted that political writing is liable to censorship in a totalitarian state, surely literature can flourish there. Which of the following arguments in support of this statement does Orwell not mention?

24 (a) a writer may express himself under cover of irony
    (b) not all writers have to be out of sympathy with the régime
    (c) writers do better work when they share the beliefs of their readers
    (d) the regime will regard much literature as ineffective
    (e) many books have no connexion with politics

53 *Orwell uses the phrase* 'prevailing orthodoxy' *twice (lines 62 and 70). Is it used in the same sense each time, or does it refer once to England and the second time to a totalitarian state?*

28 *Which of these phrases comes nearest to Orwell's* ' prevailing orthodoxy'?

(*a*) beliefs evolved and imposed by the rulers

(*b*) the most popular religion

(*c*) opinions and belief that gradually win acceptance

(*d*) the beliefs which public opinion and the government encourage you to hold

(*e*) views that happen to be held by the majority

George Orwell strongly denies that literature can flourish in a totalitarian state. He believes that the importance of any writer' work resides in his

64 (*a*) technique (*b*) audience (*c*) frankness (*d*) conviction (*e*) motives

Moreover his definition of 'political' *includes any topic which*

 6 (*a*) strongly appeals to a writer

(*b*) could not be expressed in lyric verse

(*c*) contains any implications about man and society

(*d*) can be labelled as modern

(*e*) has become a taboo

B *Give past or present examples in your own experience or knowledge of*
1. a temporary expedient 2. a theocracy 3. a ruling caste 4. a revaluation of a prominent historical figure 5. philistinism 6. a venal hack 7. a writer who 'distorts and caricatures reality in order to make his meaning clearer', but who does not 'misrepresent the scenery of his mind' 8. a taboo

C *Taking into account Orwell's ideas, write an essay on one of the following*

1. The objective truth of history
2. Is 'double-think' here already?
3. The dangers when a few rich men control the Press
4. Topics now debarred from serious discussion
5. Does literature thrive in an age of violent controversy?
6. Literature as 'a criticism of life'
7. How much freedom should journalists be permitted?
8. Can a lyric poet 'breathe' in a totalitarian state?

Further reading

PLATO, *The Republic*, trans. F. M. Cornford. Oxford University Press, 1941. Part V, 'The quarrel between Philosophy and Poetry'.

JOHN MILTON, *Areopagitica* (1644).

EDWARD CRANKSHAW, *Krushchev's Russia*. Penguin, 1960. See the chapter entitled 'The Great Thaw'.

Modern novels such as *Brave New World* by ALDOUS HUXLEY (Chatto, 1932); *1984* by GEORGE ORWELL (Secker, 1949); *Fahrenheit 451* by RAY BRADBURY (Hart-Davis, 1954).

8 The Origin of the Universe

'It's lovely to live on a raft. We had the sky, up there, all speckled with stars, and we used to lay on our backs and look up at them, and discuss about whether they was made, or only just happened – Jim he allowed they was made, but I allowed they happened; I judged it would have took too long to *make* so many. Jim said the moon could a *laid* them; well, that looked kind of reasonable, so I didn't say nothing against it, because I've seen a frog lay most as many, so of course it could be done. We used to watch the stars that fell, too, and see them streak down. Jim allowed they'd got spoiled and was hove out of the nest.'

(Mark Twain, *The Adventures of Huckleberry Finn.* 1884)

† *The Individual and the Universe,* by A. C. B. Lovell, 1961 (*broadcast in 1958*)

I have already mentioned the Abbé Lemaître. His original work in 1927, published in a little-known journal, was discovered by Eddington. Although Eddington remained faithful to this idea that the universe evolved from the static but unstable Einstein universe, the conception was soon abandoned by Lemaître himself. For the past twenty-five years Lemaître's name has been associated with another model whose origin recedes even farther back in time than the static Einstein state. Of all cosmologies, it is, perhaps, by far the most thoroughly 10 studied. We shall see later that during the last few years a tremendous clash has occurred with other opinions, but at the present time there are no known features of the observable universe which are incompatible with Lemaître's evolutionary cosmology. Lemaître's model is typical of one of the groups of theories inherent in general relativity, according to which the universe originated at a finite time in the past and expands to an infinite size at an infinite future time.

38

Perhaps we can most easily visualize this conception by taking the universe as we see it now and inquiring quite simply what might have been the situation long ago. The observations of the distant galaxies show that their light and radio emission is shifted in wavelength so that as received on the earth the light is redder and the radio waves longer in wavelength than those which are actually emitted. The interpretation of this shift is that we are separating from the galaxies at a very high speed, and that the speed of recession is about thirty-seven thousand miles per second, which is a fifth of the velocity of light. The observation which gives us this figure is of a cluster of galaxies in Hydra photographed in the two-hundred-inch telescope. The so-called cosmological principle which is inherent in Lemaître's theory implies that if human beings equipped with similar instruments existed on a planet in this Hydra cluster of galaxies, then they would see the cluster of galaxies to which we belong at the limit of their powers of observation, and the velocity of recession would also be thirty-seven thousand miles per second. It is important to rid ourselves of any idea that, because all around us we find galaxies in recession, then we are the centre of the recessional movement. This is not the case. It is an impression which we obtain because we can see only a small part of the total universe.

To return to this cluster of galaxies in Hydra. We are now seeing it as it was two thousand million years ago moving away at a rate of thirty-seven thousand miles a second. What is the likely past history of this and all other similar galaxies? Up to a point this question is not too difficult to answer. For example, a minute ago we were two million miles closer to this cluster than we are now. A year ago we were over a billion miles closer. If we recede back into history in this manner we realize that the galaxies such as Hydra which are now almost beyond our view must have been very much closer to us in the remote past. In fact, if we proceed in this way, then we reach a time of about eight or nine thousand million years ago when all the galaxies must have been very close together indeed. Of course, the galaxies themselves have evolved during this time, but the primeval material from which they were formed must have existed in a space which is very small compared with the universe today.

With important reservations which I shall deal with now, this in essence is the fundamental concept of Lemaître's theory,
60 namely, that the universe originated from a dense and small conglomerate which Lemaître calls the primeval atom. I shall return in a moment to the conditions which might have existed at the beginning, and to the possible events which might have initiated the disruption and expansion of the primeval atom. It is in fact necessary to emphasize that the theory does not demand the formation of the galaxies in the first phase of the expansion. The primeval atom contained the entire material of the universe, and its density must have been inconceivably high – at least a hundred million tons per cubic centimetre. The
70 initial momentum of the expansion dispersed this material, and after thousands of millions of years the conditions applicable to the so-called Einstein universe would have been reached. Then the size of the universe was about a thousand million light years and the density would have been comparable to that with which we are familiar on earth. According to Lemaître, at this stage the initial impetus of the expansion was nearly exhausted and the universe began to settle down into the nearly static condition which we have previously considered, where the forces of gravitational attraction and cosmical repulsion were in
80 balance. The mathematical treatment indicates that the universe must have stayed for a long time in this condition. It is during this phase that the great clusters of galaxies began to form the primeval material. Then the conditions of near equilibrium were again upset, the forces of cosmical repulsion began to win over those of gravitational attraction, and the universe was launched on the career of expansion which after nine thousand million years brought it to the state which we witness today.

The time scale determined by tracing back the past history of the galaxies brings us not to the beginning of time and space,
90 but merely to a condition which existed a few thousand million years ago when the universe was probably about one-tenth of its present size and consisted of the original gaseous clouds from which the clusters of galaxies began to form. The processes of the formation and evolution of the galaxies from this early stage are the subject of very detailed mathematical treatment. There is, at present, every reason to believe that a satisfactory explanation of the evolution of the universe from that condition can be

given in terms of the known laws of physics. But when we pass
on to consider the even earlier stages, difficulties and uncertain-
100 ties appear. How much farther do we have to go back in time
to the condition of the primeval atom? The theory does not
determine this with any precision, because the delay which the
universe suffered during the equilibrium phase when the
gaseous clouds were forming into galaxies cannot be specified.
One can, however, say this – that the explosion or disintegration of the primeval atom must have occurred between twenty
thousand million and sixty thousand million years ago. In
other words the period of about nine thousand million years
ago, when the galaxies began to form and the present period of
110 expansion began, represents a comparatively recent phase in
the history of the universe.

.   .   .

The theory which we have discussed envisages a once for all
creation in the remote past followed by a steady evolution to
the present conditions. The alternative to this theory is that the
creation of matter is taking place continuously and that although stars and galaxies evolve from this basic material, the
universe, when considered as a large-scale structure, is in a
steady state. We can illustrate this view by considering the
future history of the galaxies which are now near the limit of
120 observation. We are receding at great speed from these galaxies.
In a billion years' time the galaxies will have passed for ever
from our field of view and other galaxies which are now closer
to us will have moved out to our observable horizon. So much
is common ground on both the evolutionary and steady-state
theories. The sharp distinction arises when we compare the
picture of the universe within the observable horizon now and
in a billion years' time. On the evolutionary theory more and
more galaxies move out of our field of view, and the number of
galaxies which we can see with our instruments will for ever
130 decrease. In other words, the average spatial density of the
universe is decreasing. On the steady-state theory this is not the
case. Although individual galaxies recede beyond the observable horizon, others are always being created to take their
place. In a billion years' time the universe will look to us very
much as it does now. The individual galaxies will have changed,

but their average spatial density remains the same, because matter is always in creation throughout all of space. The cosmological principle of the evolutionary theory in which the universe would appear to be the same to any observer, wherever
140 he was situated in space, has become the perfect cosmological principle according to which the universe is the same throughout all space and time.

The implications of this point of view are, of course, profound. For example, there cannot have been a beginning in any scale of time at all. If we trace back in time the history of the galaxies, they dissolve into gas and then into uncreated matter as they move in towards us, whereas others come into view from beyond the observable horizon. At a time of twenty thousand million years ago the evolutionary models picture the universe
150 as a concentrated conglomerate of gas, whereas the steady-state universe would have appeared as it does today. Indeed, however far we go back in time, there is no stage at which we can say that the universe, as a whole, had a beginning. In the only language at our command we can say that the history of the universe on the steady-state theory extends to an infinite time in the past.

Whereas there is hope that we can put our inferences about the past to an experimental test, we can discuss the future only in terms of the predictions of cosmological theory. Here again
160 there are great differences between the evolutionary and steady-state models. The predictions of the steady-state theory are quite clear. The universe has an infinite extent in space and an infinite future in time. There is, of course, a limit to the observable universe from any one place in it determined by the speed of expansion. But if an intelligent being exists at our observable limit he would find himself surrounded by a similar universe of galaxies and so on without end. Neither does the theory of continuous creation place any limitation on the future extent in time. In the same way that a billion years ago the universe
170 would look the same as it does now, so in a billion years of future existence the overall large-scale picture will be unchanged.

The future on the evolutionary models is quite different. The total content of matter was fixed once and for all at the time of creation. The expansion is thinning out the galaxies, and in a

billion years our view of space would indeed be vastly different from what it is today. In some variations of the evolutionary theory the process of expansion is expected to reverse when the spatial density has fallen to a certain value, and then the con-
180 traction of space would bring the ageing galaxies into view again. But even in such variations of the evolutionary models the ultimate death of the universe seems inescapable, because the energy with which the universe was imbued at its creation is relentlessly becoming less available.

A *Here is a summary of Sir Bernard Lovell's account of the 'Big Bang' theory. Fill in the gaps from the words given below. No word occurs twice.*

The first theory — **21** by the writer is based on the fact, — **9** by astronomers, that the galaxies are flying apart very rapidly. Therefore there must have been a time when the galaxies were — **70** in a comparatively small space. Lemaître — **37** a very dense primeval atom which — **50** at least twenty thousand million years ago. The material eventually — **30** into comparative equilibrium for a long period, during which the galaxies — **55** out of gaseous clouds into the form that we now see. Then the disintegrating forces once more — **43** the binding forces and the galaxies — **13** to fly apart. The length of the lull cannot be precisely — **60**; all that can be — **35** is that the primeval atom must have started to disintegrate between twenty thousand and sixty thousand million years ago, and that the universe again — **73** about nine thousand million years ago – a process which is still continuing.

asserted, assigned, began, calculated, concentrated, criticized, declined, denied, doubted, established, evolved, expanded, exploded, found, happened, imagined, investigated, opposed, outlined, overcame, postulated, settled, suggested.

B
46 *The writer chooses the cluster of galaxies in Hydra as his example*

(*a*) by chance
(*b*) because Lemaître chose it

THE ORIGIN OF THE UNIVERSE

(c) because it is near the limits of vision
(d) because it travels 37,000 miles per second from us
(e) because there may be life on the galaxies in it

20 *A feature of the Einstein universe is*

(a) precarious equilibrium
(b) recession (i.e. of galaxies)
(c) stability
(d) unlimited size
(e) continuous evolution of galaxies out of gases

C *The 'Steady-state' theory*
Summarize this theory (as given in lines 114–156) in 80–100 words,
without mentioning the previous theory.

D *The next five questions refer to the last three paragraphs (lines 143–184)*

51 *The 'profound implications' (line 143) that the writer discusses concern*

(a) the accuracy of astronomical calculations
(b) the movements of the galaxies towards us
(c) the resources of language
(d) the possible existence of intelligent beings elsewhere in the universe
(e) the question whether time is finite or infinite

40 *The 'observable horizon' (line 148) refers to*

(a) the line where sky and earth meet
(b) the plane through the earth's centre which is parallel to (a)
(c) the limit of human observation
(d) the limit of imagination
(e) recorded time

5 *'Models' (line 161). Which is the word nearest in meaning?*
(a) imitations (b) rules (c) schemes (d) ideals (e) approximations

66 *To which word in the sentence (lines 153–156) does the writer particularly refer in his phrase, 'the only language at our command'?*
(a) history (b) universe (c) steady-state (d) infinite (e) past

44

31 *A fresh idea is mentioned about some, but not all, of the evolutionary theories, namely that*

    (*a*) the universe may grow smaller

    (*b*) the universe is growing less dense

    (*c*) new worlds are being created

    (*d*) our view of space is altering

    (*e*) the universe is running down

E *How relevant is radio astronomy to the conflict between the two theories? Is there any sentence in these three paragraphs which might refer to its findings?*

F *Write on the implications, as they strike you, of the two theories.*

G *What branches of science, apart from astronomy, does the writer mention as being involved in these two theories?*

H *Turn back to the conversation between Huckleberry Finn and Jim on the raft. How seriously can we take their various remarks about the stars*

    (*a*) as astronomical theories, phrased though they may be very naïvely

    (*b*) as serving to reveal two sorts of human character?

Further reading

R. A. LYTTLETON, *The Modern Universe*. Hodder and Stoughton, 1956; Arrow Books.

P. COUDERC, *The Wider Universe*. Arrow Books, 1960.

F. HOYLE, *The Nature of the Universe*. Blackwell, 1950; Pelican.

H. BONDI, W. S. BONNER, R. A. LYTTLETON and G. J. WHITRON, *Rival Theories of Cosmology*. Oxford University Press, 1960.

G. C. MCVITTIE, *Fact and Theory in Cosmology*. Eyre and Spottiswoode, 1962.

The second and last of these books are harder than the others.

9 The Real World

† *Dilemmas*, by Gilbert Ryle, 1953

When we are in a certain intellectual mood, we seem to find clashes between the things that scientists tell us about our furniture, clothes and limbs, and the things that we tell about them. We are apt to express these felt rivalries by saying that the world whose parts and members are described by scientists is different from the world whose parts and members we describe ourselves, and yet, since there can be only one world, one of these seeming worlds must be a dummy world. Moreover, as no one nowadays is hardy enough to say 'Bo' to science, it
10 must be the world that we ourselves describe which is the dummy-world.

. . .

As a preface to the serious part of the argument I want to deflate two over-inflated ideas, from which derives not the cogency but some of the persuasiveness of the argument for the irreconcilability of the world of science with the everyday world. One is the idea of *science*, the other that of *world*.

(a) There is no such animal as 'Science'. There are scores of sciences. Most of these sciences are such that acquaintance-ship with them or, what is even more captivating, hearsay
20 knowledge about them has not the slightest tendency to make us contrast their world with the everyday world. Philology is a science, but not even popularizations of its discoveries would make anyone feel that the world of philology cannot be accommodated by the world of familiar people, things and happenings. Let philologists discover everything discoverable about the structures and origins of the expressions that we use; yet their

46

discoveries have no tendency to make us write off as mere dummies the expressions that we use and that philologists also use. The sole dividedness of mind that is induced in us by learn-
30 ing any of the lessons of philology is akin to that which we sometimes experience when told, say, that our old, familiar paper-weight was once an axe-head used by a prehistoric warrior. Something utterly ordinary becomes also, just for the moment, charged with history. A mere paper-weight becomes also, just for the moment, a death-dealing weapon. But that is all.

Nor do most of the other sciences give us the feeling that we live our daily lives in a bubble-world. Botanists, entomologists, meteorologists, and geologists do not seem to threaten the walls,
40 floors and ceilings of our common dwelling-place. On the contrary, they seem to increase the quantity and improve the arrangement of its furniture. Nor even, as might be supposed, do all branches of physical science engender in us the idea that our everyday world is a dummy-world. The discoveries and theories of astronomers and astro-physicists may make us feel that the earth is very small, but only by making us feel that the heavens are very big. The gnawing suspicion that both the terrestrial and the super-terrestrial alike are merely painted stage-canvas is not begotten by even hearsay knowledge of the
50 physics of the immense. It is not begotten, either, by hearsay knowledge of the physics of the middle-sized. The theory of the pendulum, the cannon-ball, the water-pump, the fulcrum, the balloon and the steam-engine does not by itself drive us to vote between the everyday world and the so-called world of science. Even the comparatively minute can be accommodated by us without theoretical heart-searchings in our everyday world. Pollen-grains, frost-crystals and bacteria, though revealed only through the microscope, do not by themselves make us doubt whether middle-sized and immense things may not belong
60 where rainbows and mirages or even dreams belong. We always knew that there were things too small to be seen with the naked eye; the magnifying-glass and the microscope have surprised us not by establishing their existence but by disclosing their variety and, in some cases, their importance.

No, there are, I think, two branches of science which, especially when in collusion with one another, produce what I

may describe as the 'poison-pen effect', the effect of half-persuading us that our best friends are really our worst enemies. One is the physical theory of the ultimate elements of matter;
70 the other is that one wing of human physiology which investigates the mechanism and functioning of our organs of perception. I do not think it makes much difference to the issue whether these ultimate elements of matter are described as the Greek atomists described them or as the twentieth-century nuclear physicist describes them. Nor do I think that it makes much difference whether we consider old-fashioned guesses or recent conclusive discoveries about the mechanism of perception. The upsetting moral drawn by Epicurus, Galileo, Sydenham and Locke is precisely that drawn by Eddington, Sherring-
80 ton and Russell. The fact that this upsetting moral was once drawn from a piece of speculation and is now drawn from well-established scientific theory makes no difference. The moral drawn is not a piece of good science now, and it was not a piece of bad science then.

So the so-called world of science which, we gather, has the title to replace our everyday world is, I suggest, the world not of science in general but of atomic and sub-atomic physics in particular, enhanced by some slightly incongruous appendages borrowed from one branch of neuro-physiology.

90   (b) The other idea which needs prefatory deflation is that of *world*. When we hear that there is a grave disparity between our everyday world and the world of science or, a little more specifically, the world of one wing of physical science, it is difficult for us to shake off the impression that there are some physicists who by dint of their experiments, calculations and theorizing have qualified themselves to tell us everything that is really important about the cosmos, whatever that may be. Where theologians used to be the people to tell us about the creation and management of the cosmos, now these physicists are the
100 experts – for all that in the articles and books that they write for their colleagues and pupils the word 'world' seldom occurs, and the grand word 'cosmos', I hope, never occurs. There is some risk of a purely verbal muddle here. We know that a lot of people are interested in poultry and would not be surprised to find in existence a periodical called 'The Poultry World'. Here the word 'world' is not used as theologians use it. It is a

collective noun used to label together all matters pertaining to poultry-keeping. It could be paraphrased by 'field' or 'sphere of interest' or 'province'. In this use there could be no question 110 of a vendetta between the poultry world and the Christian world, since, while 'world' could be paraphrased by 'cosmos' in the phrase 'Christian world', it could not be so paraphrased in the other.

It is obviously quite innocuous to speak of the physicists' world, if we do so in the way in which we speak of the poultry-keeper's world or the entertainment world. We could correspondingly speak of the bacteriologist's world and the marine zoologist's world. In this use there is no connotation of cosmic authority, for the word 'world' in this use does not mean '*the* 120 world' or 'the cosmos'. On the contrary, it means the *department* of interests which physicists' interests constitute.

But this is not the whole story. For while there are hosts of interests, scientific, political, artistic, etc., from which the interests peculiar to physicists are distinguished, while, that is, there are hosts of provinces of interest, which are different from without being rivals of the physicist's province, there remains an important respect in which the subject-matters of fundamental physical theory do comprehend or cover the subject-matters of all the other natural sciences. The specimens col- 130 lected by the marine biologist, though of no special interest to the physical theorist, are still, in an indirect way, specimens of what he is specially interested in. So too are the objects studied by the geologist, the mycologist and the philatelist. There is nothing that any natural scientist studies of which the truths of physics are not true; and from this it is tempting to infer that the physicist is therefore talking about everything, and so that he is, after all, talking about the cosmos. So, after all, the cosmos must be described only in his terms, and can only be mis-described in the terms of any of these other more special sciences, 140 or, more glaringly, in theological terms, or, most glaringly of all, in the terms of everyday conversation.

Let me remind you that, just as a little while ago I was not finding fault with economic theory when I argued that it told neither lies nor the truth about my brother's character, so I am not now finding fault with the theories of physicists when I argue that they tell neither lies nor the truth about the world, in

any awe-inspiring sense of 'the world'. Just as I then argued
that economic theory, without mentioning my brother, told the
truth about any marketing-transactions that he or anyone else
150 might engage in, so I am now arguing that the truths of fundamental physical theory are, without mentioning the cosmos,
truths about anything whatsoever in the world.

Least of all am I trying to expound or contribute to any
scientific theory. I have not got the competence and, if I had, I
hope that I would not have the inclination. My sole concern is
to show how certain non-scientific morals seem to be but are
not consequential upon a certain sort of scientific theory. I am
questioning nothing that any scientist says on weekdays in his
working tone of voice. But I certainly am questioning most of
160 what a very few of them say in an edifying tone of voice on
Sundays.

I am now going to try to bring out the underlying logical
pattern of the view that the truths of physical theory leave no
room for the truths of daily life, and this I do by means of a
long-drawn-out analogy with which I hope you will bear for
some little time. An undergraduate member of a college is one
day permitted to inspect the college accounts and to discuss
them with the auditor. He hears that these accounts show how
the college has fared during the year. 'You will find', he is
170 told, 'that all the activities of the college are represented in these
columns. Undergraduates are taught, and here are the tuition-
fees that they pay. Their instructors teach, and here are the
stipends that they receive. Games are played, and here are the
figures; so much for rent of the ground, so much for the wages
of the groundsman, and so on. Even your entertainments are
recorded; here is what was paid out to the butchers, grocers
and fruiterers, here are the kitchen-charges, and here is what
you paid in your college battels.' At first the undergraduate is
merely mildly interested. He allows that these columns give him
180 a different sort of view of the life of the college from the patch-
work quilt of views that he had previously acquired from his
own experiences of working in the library, playing football,
dining with his friends, and the rest. But then under the influence
of the auditor's grave and sober voice he suddenly begins to
wonder. Here everything in the life of the college is systema-
tically marshalled and couched in terms which, though colourless,

are precise, impersonal and susceptible of conclusive checking. To every plus there corresponds an equal and opposite
minus; the entries are classified; the origins and destinations of
190 all payments are indicated. Moreover, a general conclusion is
reached; the financial position of the college is exhibited and
compared with its position in previous years. So is not this
expert's way, perhaps, the right way in which to think of the life
of the college, and the other muddled and emotionally charged
ways to which he had been used the wrong ways?

At first in discomfort he wriggles and suggests 'May not these
accounts give us just one part of the life of the college? The
chimney-sweep and the inspector of electricity-meters see their
little corners of the activities of the college; but no one supposes
200 that what they have to tell is more than a petty fragment of
the whole story. Perhaps you, the auditor, are like them and see
only a small part of what is going on.' But the auditor rejects
this suggestion. 'No,' he says, 'here are the payments to the
chimney-sweep at so much per chimney swept, and here are
the payments to the Electricity Board at so much a unit. Everybody's part in the college life, including my own, is down here
in figures. There is nothing departmental in the college accounts.
Everything is covered. What is more, the whole system of
accountancy is uniform for all colleges and is, at least in general
210 pattern, uniform for all businesses, government departments
and town councils. No speculations or hypotheses are admitted;
our results are lifted above the horizons of opinion and prejudice by the sublime Principle of Double Entry. These accounts tell the objective truth about the entire life of the whole
college; the stories that you tell about it to your brothers and
sisters are only picturesque travesties of the audited facts. They
are only dreams. Here are the realities.' What is the undergraduate to reply? He cannot question the accuracy, compre-
hensiveness or exhaustiveness of the accounts. He cannot com-
220 plain that they cover five or six sides of college life, but do not
cover the other sixteen sides. All the sides that he can think of
are indeed duly covered.

Perhaps he is acute enough to suspect that there has been
some subtle trick played by this word 'covered'. The tuition
he had received last term from the lecturer in Anglo-Saxon was
indeed covered, yet the accounts were silent about what had

been taught and the auditor betrayed no inquisitiveness about what progress the student had made. He, too, the under-graduate himself, had been covered in scores of sections of the accounts, as a recipient of an Exhibition, as a pupil of the lec-turer in Anglo-Saxon and so on. He had been covered, but not characterized or mischaracterized. Nothing was said about him that would not have fitted a much taller Exhibitioner or a much less enthusiastic student of Anglo-Saxon. Nothing had been said about him personally at all. He has not been de-scribed, though he has been financially accounted for.

Take a special case. In one way the auditor is very much interested in the books that the librarian buys for the college library. They must be scrupulously accounted for, the price paid for each must be entered, the fact of the actual receipt of the book must be recorded. But in another way the auditor need not be at all interested in these books, since he need not have any idea what the books contain or whether anybody reads them. For him the book is merely what is indicated by the price mark on its jacket. For him the differences between one book and another are differences in shillings. The figures in the sec-tion devoted to library accounts do indeed cover every one of the actual books bought; yet nothing in these figures would have been different had these books been different in subject-matter, language, style and binding, so long as their prices were the same. The accounts tell neither lies nor the truth about the contents of any of the books. In the reviewer's sense of 'describe', they do not describe any of the books, though they scrupulously cover all of the books.

Which, now, is the real and which the bubble-book, the book read by the undergraduate or the book whose price is entered in the library-accounts? Clearly there is no answer. There are not two books, nor yet one real book, side by side with another bubble-book – the latter, queerly, being the one that is useful for examinations. There is just a book available for students, and an entry in the accounts specifying what the college paid for it. There could not be a library stocked with mere book-prices; though also there could not be a well-conducted college which had a library full of books but required no library accounts to be kept.

The library used by the student is the same library as that

accounted for by the accountant. What the student finds in the library is what the accountant tells the pounds, shillings and pence of. I am suggesting, you see, that it is in partially the same
270 way that the world of the philologist, the marine-biologist, the astronomer and the housewife is the same world as that of the physicist; and what the pedestrian and the bacteriologist find in the world is what the physicist tells him about in his double-entry notation.

A *Here is a summary of paragraphs 3–6 (lines 17–89). Pick the right word for each gap.*

Science is not a single entity but a number of — **34** [linked/ separate/conflicting/fascinating/incompatible] sciences. It is rare for any of these sciences to reveal an — **54** [everyday/ exciting/elementary/alternate/alternative] world that in any way — **7** [conflicts with/supports/disposes of/ridicules/contradicts] the — **59** [familiar/trivial/real/unchanging/known] world. To take one example, the science of philology could not even be imagined as hostile to the ordinary world; it may impart a — **22** [salutary/profound/shattering/temporary/rude] shock when we are suddenly made to take a fresh look at a phrase that is — **72** [trite/hackneyed/much-used/expressive/old-fashioned], but it does not affect the — **39** [history/power/importance/ meaning/significance] of that phrase.

So far from undermining our world, most sciences fortify it. Moreover, most of the physical sciences themselves support it. At one extreme, astronomy and astro-physics make us — **14** [distort/evolve/doubt/accept/re-adjust] our — **57** [scale/system/ method/sense/instruments] of measurement outside the earth but not on it; near the other extreme, the microscope, by showing things too small for the naked eye, has — **17** [denied/corroborated/disproved/claimed/magnified] what we have always known and has — **67** [terrified/alarmed/deceived/disillusioned/startled] us only by the amount revealed; and an interest in the physics of intermediate objects depends on their — **27** [potential/ precise/practicable/practical/simple] uses.

What on the contrary makes us doubt the reality of our world is the — **44** [combination/implication/conflict/culmination/ corroboration] of two sciences—physics (both atomic and sub-atomic) and that part of physiology which tells us how we perceive things. This is no — **2** [sudden/inexplicable/ancient/unexpected/modern] phenomenon. Frequently in the past have these two sciences together produced — **47** [disconcerting/discredited/novel/attractive/conclusive] theories of the type that now also make people think that the everyday world is — **32** [fascinating/mysterious/incomprehensible/a replacement/illusory].

B *Distinguish between the meanings of the word* 'world' *in the following*

63   The world is too much with us; late and soon,
       Getting and spending, we lay waste our powers;
       Little we see in Nature that is ours.

18   God be thanked, the meanest of his creatures
       Boasts two soul-sides, one to face the world with,
       One to show a woman when he loves her!

48 Bishop Berkeley destroyed this world in one volume octavo; and nothing remained, after his time, but mind; which experienced a similar fate from the hand of Mr Hume in 1737.

25   Ye gods, it doth amaze me,
       A man of such a feeble temper should
       So get the start of the majestic world,
       And bear the palm alone.
                [Cassius of Julius Caesar]

52   . . . oft a flood
       Have we two wept, and so
       Drowned the whole world, us two.
                  [Of two lovers]

10 'The world of sound' (a phrase used by the BBC)

C *Write sentences of your own to illustrate the various meanings that these words might carry*: life, nature, science, real, material

D *Express in not more than thirty words why it is that physics speaks with more extensive authority than, say, bacteriology.*

E *The passage ends with a long analogy. Translate it back so that it directly refers to the seeming collision between the world of physics and the everyday world. You may find this a useful way to begin*:
'A student one day is introduced to the theory of ultimate

particles. He is told that this theory accounts for every material feature of the life around him – substances, objects, living creatures – and that everything can thus be reduced to fixed units of measurement. At first the student is only mildly interested. This is, he sees, a novel way of looking at the world, unlike what he is used to from his own various experiences. But . . .

F *What moments in the analogy do you find most amusing? Do the humorous touches themselves add further point to the analogy?*

G *Show how it is possible for either* Economics *or* Psychology *to give an account of man's true nature that contradicts our ordinary view.*

If you can, invent an analogy that deflates their pretensions and restores proportion.

H *What do you think is Ryle's attitude to* Theology? *Is there anything surprising in the eleventh paragraph (beginning 'Least of all . . .')? Did it alter your view of Ryle's purpose?*

10 The Problem of Suffering

Introduction by Margaret E. Rose to *The Problem of Suffering*, 1962

[First heading]

A detached and rational look at the universe does not immediately suggest that behind it there is a good and compassionate God; rather the opposite. The vastness even of the known universe, and the smallness of the area in which life is possible, make life appear accidental and man puny and insignificant. The forms of life which appear prey upon each other, and man's achievement of self-consciousness appears to have involved him in more pain than animals and more power to inflict pain. Civilizations arise and struggle towards a knowledge of truth and
10 a better way of life; but in time pass away and are succeeded by others, not necessarily superior. And although a measure of the suffering which all this involves may be said to strengthen character, many of the evils which beset us – earthquakes, concentration camps, mental and moral deficiency – provide ruthless situations in which personalities are crushed rather than strengthened. And those who point to some kind of eternal justice behind the happenings of history appear to be confounded by the enormous permission given to the evil strong man to torture and destroy.
20 Thoughts like these have led many people to deny that there is anything meaningful behind the universe at all; or even, like Thomas Hardy, to assert that what powers there are are malevolent towards man. For these, at least, the issue is clear-cut;

there is tragedy, but no intellectual problem. The problem arises for those who assert that, in spite of appearances, the power behind the universe is 'good'. Given the facts as we know them, perhaps the most astonishing fact of all is that innumerable men of all places and periods should have postulated and believed in a good God. Yet this 'universal hope'
30 appears to be ineradicable. There is something in human nature which can only see meaning in that which it recognizes to be good.

Whoever takes his stand on the belief that what is behind the universe is good and beneficent to man is indeed faced with a problem. The argument which he will have to answer runs something like this: 'If God were good, he would wish to make his creatures happy. If God were almighty, he would be able to do what he wished.' The believer will then need to question whether happiness is indeed the ultimate end of man
40 and of what kind it should be. He will need to inquire what is meant by the almightiness or omnipotence of God, and to point out that even God cannot carry out two mutually exclusive alternatives. That is to say, if he gives freedom to his creatures, he must allow them to choose evil as well as good, and make such conditions as will enable them to have such a choice. And if the same God makes a universal order governed by certain laws, if his universe is to be rational and predictable, he will not be able perpetually to intervene between cause and effect, in order to be able to promote this individual happiness or
50 prevent that calamity. The believer may be driven to say that some evil is only apparent; that man judges by a scale of values different from God's; and that the purposes of God transcend the finite world and cannot be explained wholly in terms of it. He will find it difficult to provide an answer to his problem which is wholly satisfying to the intellect. If an answer exists, it lies elsewhere and is of another kind.

[Second heading]

The later history of religious ideas and controversies is largely the history of man's struggle with this problem. For primitive man, living in a world of good and evil spirits, there was no
60 philosophical problem; only an urgent need to placate the gods and spirits with charms and incantations, and sacrificial cere-

monies by which guilt could be transferred or destroyed which might otherwise be punishable by disaster. The gods of the Greeks were also numerous and amoral. But in the plays of Euripides, Aeschylus, and Sophocles human suffering as a tragic fact (not a problem in our sense) is central. And two ideas emerge which seem to grope after what was later to be said more clearly: (1) the idea of the sufferer who is also a pain-bearer for others; and (2) the idea of a moral law behind the
70 universe which would inexorably punish men for 'hubris' (arrogance) or 'pleonexia' (greed).

The Persian people observed that both good and evil forces were at work in the universe, and portrayed the situation as a gigantic battleground between powers of light and powers of darkness, in which man was caught up and involved. Zoroaster taught that man could assist in bringing about the victory of the powers of light. These dualist ideas had a far-reaching influence; they have always attracted people as a compara-tively easy way of exonerating a good God from any responsi-
80 bility for evil things. But in effect they dethrone God, and drive the problem of the origin of evil one stage farther back.

The people who first seemed to understand intuitively that God, in order truly to be God, must be God of the whole creation, responsible for all creation and controlling the pur-poses of life, were the Hebrews. From a chaos of superstitions and narrow ideas of a warlike tribal God, there emerged a monotheistic creed, inconsistent with dualism. This God of the Hebrews, according to their later prophets, was the only God; he was righteous and holy. How, then, could they account for
90 the disasters which overtook their nation, or which overtook apparently innocent people? For a long period, the more secure and conventional Hebrew saw suffering only as a punish-ment for sin. But throughout Hebrew literature there perpetu-ally emerge rebellious, honest, or tender thinkers – who know that this solution to the problem is too easy, is in fact a lie, and will not abide in it. And although they bow their heads before ultimate mystery and find personal satisfaction in faith – they do not provide an 'answer' intelligible to the unbelieving. Later
100 ideas in Hebrew thinking move two ways. Some move back-wards towards the idea of an 'Evil One' in a new dualism; and

one writer – the anonymous author of the 'Servant Songs' at the end of the Book of Isaiah – gropes towards the idea of suffering as a means of 'redemption'.

The idea that suffering, though itself not good, might, by the acceptance of it by a good person, be the means of transforming this person and others: the idea of dying to be re-born, of becoming a sacrifice on which others may feed – both these ideas, which had emerged many times in crude ceremony or
110 purer thought, were to be renewed and fulfilled in the life and death of Christ, as the early Christian Church understood it. It is perhaps the most remarkable phenomenon in the history of religious thought, that when the early Christians looked back and pondered the doing to death of Jesus Christ, it did not reduce them to despair, but seemed to them to show forth the redeeming love of God. The crucifixion seems to reduce to absurdity belief in a world governed by a gracious providence. Men in the Old Testament had been staggered and shaken by the sufferings of the righteous. Why did not the first Christians
120 feel the same about Jesus? They seemed to understand that he had conformed himself to the pattern of the redeeming Servant and to the will of God: and their testimony was that on Easter morning they encountered him as one who had in some way 'overcome' sin and suffering as well as death.

Christians, believing that God had become incarnate in his own creation, were prepared to say that there was nothing inherently evil in the flesh itself, but that human beings had 'gone astray' and made it necessary for God to intervene to redeem them. But on the borders of Christianity at the time of
130 the early Church were a considerable number of people – Neoplatonists, Gnostics, Manichees – who believed that all evil and suffering were bound up with the body and with the material world. In this they agreed with the teachings of the Buddha, who, six hundred years before in India, had propounded a 'way' in which man might escape from suffering by escaping from the need to be reborn into mortal life. The Buddha, however, who did not postulate a God and remained agnostic as far as the ultimate meaning and purpose of the universe was concerned, faced a limited metaphysical problem. But the Gnostics and
140 similar sects fell into a new kind of dualism by believing in a pure God of the realms of the spirit, and an evil Demiurge who,

falling from the world of spirit, created a world of matter which was wholly evil.

It is easier to accept the position of those who, while not supposing the material world to be evil, believed that our present finite condition of growth or 'becoming' would give rise to necessary imperfections both in the material universe and in man's nature. Such a point of view was held by Leibnitz and by William Blake, who talks of man as a free spirit 'shrunk up'
150 into his present material form but able to use this experience and the suffering involved in it for good ends. And both ultimately put their faith in the Christian idea of redemption, an idea which presupposes certain definite things about the character of God and the character of men which need to be examined. In order to test the Christian gospel of redemption, it is necessary to ask certain questions, not only about the nature of God, but about the nature of man. What is man like and what is he for?

[Third heading]

It is perhaps not unnatural that when men have tried to sum up
160 human nature and the human situation, the view which they have expressed has often not been a balanced one, and there has been a tendency to talk in terms of extreme pessimism or extreme optimism. The literature of our own age inclines towards pessimism – a sense of angry disillusionment that man is as bad as he is. Others, however, take an optimistic point of view. Man, they say, is not inherently evil at all. Scientific knowledge, which is giving him adequate material resources, comfort, leisure, greater freedom from disease, will solve his problems and bring about his 'salvation'. Change his environ-
170 ment, give him material happiness and security, and the 'evil' in man will disappear. This is the idea underlying many of the old Utopian romances – Morris's *News from Nowhere* and H. G. Wells's *Modern Utopia*. It is part of the idea underlying Marxist/ materialist states. Aldous Huxley in his book *Brave New World* painted a picture of such a state, carried to its logical conclusion. It was a perfectly planned state from which freedom, difficulty, pain, and insecurity had all disappeared. But too much comfort, too much order, too much pleasure, and a total lack of anxiety had dehumanized the people in it – they had

180 become less than human. Until at last the one rebel in the state cries out to its governor:

'I don't want comfort, I want God, I want poetry, I want real danger, I want freedom, I want goodness. I want sin.' 'In fact,' said the governor, 'you're claiming the right to be unhappy.'

Whether or not this is a true picture, whether or not men can be made too 'happy', it certainly seems that they can be made too secure. There is something in the nature of some men which makes them escape from secure situations into polar expedi-
190 tions, mountain climbing, or experiences like the Kon-Tiki adventure. It seems that the giving of material security to man will not only not make him 'good', but will not even make him happy.

Others, again, believe that what needs to be changed is not man's environment but his inner consciousness. When Darwin's ideas of progress were flourishing in a popular form at the end of the last century, it was believed by many that man was progressing 'automatically' towards a state of perfection. Two world wars have been enough to modify views about inevitable
200 progress towards wisdom and perfection. There remains the belief that man, in spite of his record of violence and wickedness, has within him potential goodness, if only this can be released. Many psychologists hold that what is needed is to set man free from fear and guilt and tension; that if he can be freed from the hidden complexes which warp his nature and left at liberty, he will then achieve wisdom and goodness. Other psychologists, however, Dr Jung among them, believe that only some 'transforming symbol', as they call it, to which a man can give reverence and worship, can ultimately make him whole.
210 At this point the Christian view of man and that of the Jungian psychologist meet; but as to the nature of man in general, fundamentally they differ. The Christian view of man is that he is 'fallen', 'self-centred', having a flaw in his nature which only some act of power and grace from beyond himself (a redemptive act on the part of God) can ultimately put right.

Which of these opinions about man's nature is the true one we can only discover by an honest study of experience – in history and society, and, perhaps more significantly, within ourselves. If we decide that man can be made 'whole' by giving

61

220 him material satisfaction, then we shall put our faith in economic and political measures to bring this about. If we believe
that what he needs is psychological release from tension, then
we shall promote the cause of psychoanalysis and try to effect
a 'cure of souls' of this kind. But if we feel that these methods
may make a man too soft, too secure, to be a full human being,
we may begin to see pain, suffering, and the tensions which they
produce in a different light. In considering the problem of
suffering in relation to the nature of man, we shall have to ask
whether some forms of suffering might even be of value to man.

[Fourth heading]

230 It seems that a slick world of painless functioning would not be
ideal for man. Only if pleasure is the supreme value could we
contemplate a painless world. If 'goodness' is that for which
man was intended, then learning through suffering and insecurity may be necessary or, at least, valuable. It is not that
the Christian view of life demands that we should regard suffering as 'a good in itself'. It is rather that the Christian, seeing a
suffering world through which a man may be able to learn to be
'made perfect', is able more easily (at least in part) to accept it.

When religious teachers talk of a way of acceptance, what
240 they mean is something more positive than resignation. They
mean that the experience of suffering and struggle and tension
and pain is necessary for growth and, if accepted as such, may
be used creatively. This is something which cannot ultimately
be tested by logic but only understood as experience. The
ancient Chinese book, the *Tao Te Ching*, expresses it like this:

> When one looks at it, one cannot see it.
> When one listens to it, one cannot hear it.
> When one uses it, it is inexhaustible.

Poets and artists have affirmed that in order to realize their
250 creative powers it was necessary to suffer. T. S. Eliot uses
Shakespeare's words: 'Those are pearls that were his eyes' to
suggest how costly the creative process is likely to be; to suggest
that works of art (the pearls) may cost artists everything that is
most precious to them. Christians of all times, following the
teaching of Christ, have affirmed that growth in goodness is a
costly process, necessitating pain and sacrifice. Blake puts this

as well as any, in describing the virtue of understanding. 'If God is anything, he is understanding. . . . Understanding is acquired by means of suffering or distress or experience. Will, 260 desire, love, pain, envy, etc., are all natural. But understanding is acquired.'

A Zen Buddhist master put even more strongly the need to accept this kind of experience and use it. When he was asked how to escape from the raging heat of finite pain, he said: 'Escape into the midst of the boiling water, into the midst of the burning fire.'

Even the kind of suffering known so well to people of all religions – the sense of blank uncertainty, the apparently un-answered prayer for guidance, the total lack of ultimate know-270 ledge of the mystery behind the chaos of experience – these things which must be a stumbling-block to the logician, may be of value to the man of faith. Faith is not certainty. It is an act of will, an act of allegiance, an act of imagination – involving a journey in the dark. It is perhaps significant how many of the heroes of myth and legend set forth on their travels without any knowledge of where they were going or even why – Odys-seus, Gawaine in the Grail story, Frodo in *The Lord of the Rings*, to name only a few. And their setting out in a state of unknow-ing is taken itself to be a virtue. 'The goodliest knowing of 280 God', says St Denis of France, 'is that which is known by unknowing.'

'Willingness to be insecure is the ultimate security.' The per-son who is able to face and use creatively even the most chaotic and destructive situation is secure against unhappiness. One of the most witty and touching examples of such an attitude is to be found in Joyce Cary's book *The Horse's Mouth*. At the end of it, the artist Gully Jimson is seen painting with complete joy and preoccupation a mural on a chapel wall, while demolition men at the other end are beginning to knock the wall down. The 290 point is only partly a sardonic one; it is also a portrayal of an act of faith and of a man whom suffering has taught to take and use time creatively, whatever the circumstances.

[*Fifth heading*]

It may perhaps be said with some justice that this is a philo-sophy for the 'spiritual aristocrat', the creative artist, the mys-

tic, or the saint; but what about the dumb millions who suffer
with little hope of ultimate benefit – the beasts of the animal
kingdom, the mental defective, the illiterate, the person whose
heredity and environment have reduced him to near non-
humanity? We may still be inclined to sympathize with Ivan
300 Karamazov when he said that if the universe had involved
acute suffering for only one child, and he as God had foreseen
that this would be so, he would not have created it.

Furthermore, from the time of the Hebrew psalmists on-
wards, men have cried out on behalf of themselves, and of
others, not just at suffering, but at the injustice of suffering, its
maldistribution, its falling alike on the guilty and innocent.
How could a righteous God – leaving mercy for a moment out
of account – so fail to vindicate the righteous? There are various
answers which can be made and which are certainly partly
310 valid. If God seeks to make men 'good' for the sake of goodness,
then he must so arrange things that reward and punishment do
not follow too automatically on good and evil action; otherwise
men might do what they did merely out of greed for reward or
fear of punishment. Moreover, it is arguable that in the long run
the universe is not indifferent to goodness. Wickedness in the
end is seen to breed wickedness, to contain the seed of self-
destruction, not to 'work'.

Meanwhile, innocent and guilty suffer together. Could this
be otherwise? If God's ultimate purpose is that man should
320 freely choose goodness, he must allow conditions of natural
evil – otherwise there would be no temptation; and he must
allow free will – otherwise man could not freely choose; but this
allows the possibility of his choosing evil which he has so often
done. And if man has to grow in goodness, he must live in a
world of growth, a world of 'becoming', a world of birth and
reproduction and death. The Buddha was right in asserting
that these conditions of mortality or 'becoming' inevitably
involve suffering. The question really is: is such suffering wholly
evil, or is it acceptable as a means to a greater good? We come
330 back to Ivan Karamazov who answered that it was not acceptable to him. But had he any right to answer that, even for himself personally? Is any human person in a position to weigh the
ultimate good or otherwise of creation? This is surely what God
meant when he spoke to Job out of the whirlwind and said:

'Where wast thou when I laid the foundations of the earth?
Declare if thou hast understanding.'

Maybe we could accept the idea of the fiery trial of human
existence more easily, if we believed that at the end of it every
suffering soul would achieve the stature of divine goodness.
340 This again is among the unknowables. And even a merciful
Christ seemed to allow that those stubborn souls who used their
freedom to deny God and stay apart from him might in the end
be 'lost'. People who do not believe in a medieval hell may still
be distressed that a 'loving' God could contemplate the eternal
damnation of any soul. But here we draw near to the heart of
the matter. A loving God is not a weakly sentimental and kindly
God: but one determined *at all costs* to himself and to man to
raise man to his full stature. When poets and saints have tried
to describe the love of God, they have turned often to the image
350 of fire – as T. S. Eliot in 'Little Gidding':

> Who then devised the torment? Love.
> Love is the unfamiliar name
> Behind the hands which wove
> The intolerable shirt of flame
> Which human power cannot remove.
> We only live, only suspire,
> Consumed by either fire, or fire.

There is no philosophical argument that can demonstrate the
truth of this: there is only revelation on God's side, and ex-
360 perience on ours. The Christian revelation proclaims not that
God in some remote impersonal way weighed the pros and cons
of creation and decided that, in spite of suffering, it could be
part of his good purpose. It proclaims that he created the world
out of love, and out of love was prepared himself to suffer in it
and for it. This, experienced as reality, is perhaps the only
'argument' which can silence the rebelliousness of man and
turn his energy to creative purpose. 'The Son of God suffered
unto death', says George Macdonald, 'not that men might *not*
suffer, but that their sufferings might be like his.'

A   *The sections of this essay have the following titles (given here in
alphabetical order)*
(*a*)   Can suffering ever be said to have value?

(*b*) Man's insight into the purposes of God
(*c*) The growth of man's idea about the nature of the universe
(*d*) The problem
(*e*) Various ideas about the nature of man

48 *Which of the above is [First heading]?*

21 „   „   „   *[Second heading]?*

61 „   „   „   *[Third heading]?*

38 „   „   „   *[Fourth heading]?*

 5 „   „   „   *[Fifth heading]?*

B *Which lines in the last four sections of the essay correspond to, or develop, each of these points in the first section?*

55 'A measure of the suffering . . . may be said to strengthen character' (*lines 11–12*).

23 'Some kind of eternal justice behind the happenings of history' (*lines 16–17*).

74 'The believer will then need to question whether happiness is indeed the ultimate end of man and of what kind it should be' (*lines 38–40*).

31 'If he gives freedom to his creatures, he must allow them to choose evil as well as good' (*lines 43–44*).

87 'The purposes of God transcend the finite world and cannot be explained wholly in terms of it' (*lines 52–53*).

12 'If an answer exists, it lies elsewhere and is of another kind' (*lines 55–56*).

C

68 *Who, besides Hardy, are said by the writer to have believed that some at least of the powers behind the Universe were bad?*

27 'The idea of the sufferer who is also a pain-bearer for others' (*lines 68–69*). *Where else is this idea found?*

42 'The idea of a moral law behind the universe which would inexorably punish men for "hubris" or "pleonexia"' (*lines 69–70*). *Where in this essay do we hear of others who took this view? And which sentence in the last section of the essay gives a philosophical objection to this idea?*

D *Here is a possible summary of the third section of the essay. Choose the best of the alternatives given for each numbered gap.*

There is an — **3** [illogical/understandable/innate/unnatural] lack of balance in man's assessment of his own nature. Modern writers — **77** [deprecate/depreciate/disillusion/destroy] man's worth; but in other periods it has been fashionable to imply that man was — **32** [basically/originally/materially/romantically] good and only needed — **50** [scientific/salvationist/enlightened/material] benefits to rise above evil. Yet a wholly — **70** [secure/logical/happy/free] environment may rob man of his true — **8** [rebellion/individuality/comfort/concern] and so — **36** [engender/admit/stifle/ensue] neither goodness nor happiness. Other — **85** [likely/Utopian/superficial/optimistic] views were that by — **17** [war/wisdom/evolution/consciousness] man himself was constantly becoming better, and that by — **45** [shrewd/complex/psychological/potential] understanding man could be — **66** [raised/liberated/shocked/transformed] from those emotions that warped his nature. Indeed some psychologists — **16** [stressing/healing/having/proving] man's need to reverence something outside — **81** [life/symbols/worship/himself], come near to the Christian view, though in making — **30** [God/man/self/nature] rather than — **90** [God/man/self/nature] their centre they differ from Christians. Only by studying man's experience can we decide whether our need is to — **13** [strengthen/test/relieve/increase] man (either by — **58** [social/curative/worldly/faithful] measures without or by — **34** [analytical/soulful/therapeutic/political] measures within) or whether — **62** [cure/challenge/release/humanity] and tension may themselves be a means of — **9** [security/value/growth/suffering].

E *Summarize the fourth section of the essay in about 100 words.*

F *Which quotation in this essay do you find most illuminating? And which do you find most obscure? Why?*

G *(Research)*
Give some account of the ideas of one writer mentioned in this essay.

H *Here are preliminary notes for an essay on Job's problem.*
Introduction. Hebrew approach (poetry, repetition, concrete rather than abstract, etc.).

1. '*Pain is punishment*' *(Comforters)*. Partially true. Misuse of

nature, health, God-given pleasures is often checked by pain (e.g. soil erosion, venereal disease, unpopularity through selfishness).

2. '*Pain is testing*' (*Satan*). 'Doth Job serve God for naught?' When the prizes are removed, one can see how deep the religion goes.

3. '*Pain is discipline*' (*Elihu*). Enlarges sympathy, purifies spirit. (Penitent Thief.) Cf. gold and dross. But it can have opposite effect.

4. '*Pain is part of a plan that we cannot fathom*' (*The Almighty*). Cf. the minnow disturbed by tides in the creek, or the child not understanding the jab in the arm.

Conclusion. Four valid points are touched on; yet no 'solution', and main point of poem is strenuous protest against the first view.

EITHER *use these notes to write the essay* Job's Problem OR *make your own notes for an essay on* God and Pain *and write the essay.*

I *This essay was originally a broadcast talk. Write a talk, to be given to the same audience the following week, on* The Problem of Sin.

11 Man and Nature

And I have felt
A presence that disturbs me with the joy
Of elevated thoughts; a sense sublime
Of something far more deeply interfused,
Whose dwelling is the light of setting suns,
And the round ocean and the living air,
And the blue sky, and in the mind of man:
A motion and a spirit, that impels
All thinking things, all objects of all thought,
And rolls through all things.

(William Wordsworth, Lines Composed a Few Miles above Tintern
Abbey)

A *What pleasure do you derive from the country? Try to distinguish between genuine pleasure and the pleasure that you assume that you will gain.*

OR: *Describe the wildest piece of scenery that you have ever seen. Try to convey in your description your feelings, for instance, of exhilaration, awe, indifference or revulsion. Do not state what this feeling is but allow the reader to deduce it from your description.*

I

† *Wordsworth in the Tropics*, by Aldous Huxley [*written before* 1936]

In the neighbourhood of latitude fifty north and for the last hundred years or thereabouts, it has been an axiom that Nature is divine and morally uplifting. For good Wordsworthians – and most serious-minded people are now Wordsworthians, either by direct inspiration or at second hand – a walk in the country is the equivalent of going to church, a tour through Westmorland is as good as a pilgrimage to Jerusalem. To commune with the fields and waters, the woodlands and the hills, is to commune, according to our modern and northern ideas, with

10   the visible manifestations of the 'Wisdom and Spirit of the Universe'.

The Wordsworthian who exports this pantheistic worship of Nature to the tropics is liable to have his religious convictions somewhat rudely disturbed. Nature, under a vertical sun, and nourished by the equatorial rains, is not at all like that chaste, mild deity who presides over the Gemuthlichkeit, the prettiness, the cosy sublimities of the Lake District. The worst that Wordsworth's goddess ever did to him was to make him hear

> Low breathings coming after me, and sounds
20   Of undistinguishable motion, steps
> Almost as silent as the turf they trod;

was to make him realize, in the shape of 'a huge peak, black and huge', the existence of 'unknown modes of being'. He seems to have imagined that this was the worst Nature could do. A few weeks in Malaya or Borneo would have undeceived him. Wandering in the hothouse darkness of the jungle, he would not have felt so serenely certain of those 'Presences of Nature', those 'Souls of Lonely Places', which he was in the habit of worshipping on the shores of Windermere and Rydal. The sparse
30   inhabitants of the equatorial forest are all believers in devils. When one has visited, in even the most superficial manner, the places where they live, it is difficult not to share their faith. The jungle is marvellous, fantastic, beautiful; but it is also terrifying, it is also profoundly sinister. There is something in what, for lack of a better word, we must call the character of great forests – even in those of temperate lands – which is foreign, appalling, fundamentally and utterly inimical to intruding man. The life of those vast masses of swarming vegetation is alien to the human spirit and hostile to it. Meredith,
40   in his 'Woods of Westermain', has tried reassuringly to persuade us that our terrors are unnecessary, that the hostility of these vegetable forces is more apparent than real, and that if we will but trust Nature we shall find our fears transformed into serenity, joy, and rapture. This may be sound philosophy in the neighbourhood of Dorking; but it begins to be dubious even in the forests of Germany – there is too much of them for a human being to feel himself at ease within their enormous glooms; and when the woods of Borneo are substituted for

those of Westermain, Meredith's comforting doctrine becomes
50 frankly ridiculous.

It is not the sense of solitude that distresses the wanderer in
equatorial jungles. Loneliness is bearable enough – for a time,
at any rate. There is something actually rather stimulating and
exciting about being in an empty place where there is no life
but one's own. Taken in reasonably small doses, the Sahara
exhilarates, like alcohol. Too much of it, however (I speak, at
any rate, for myself), has the depressing effect of the second
bottle of Burgundy. But in any case it is not loneliness that
oppresses the equatorial traveller: it is too much company; it is
60 the uneasy feeling that he is an alien in the midst of an innumerable throng of hostile beings. To us who live beneath a
temperate sky and in the age of Henry Ford, the worship of
Nature comes almost naturally. It is easy to love a feeble and
already conquered enemy. But an enemy with whom one is still
at war, an unconquered, unconquerable, ceaselessly active
enemy – no; one does not, one should not, love him. One
respects him, perhaps; one has a salutary fear of him; and one
goes on fighting. In our latitudes the hosts of Nature have
mostly been vanquished and enslaved. Some few detachments,
70 it is true, still hold the field against us. There are wild woods
and mountains, marshes and heaths, even in England. But they
are there only on sufferance, because we have chosen, out of our
good pleasure, to leave them their freedom. It has not been
worth our while to reduce them to slavery. We love them
because we are the masters, because we know that at any
moment we can overcome them as we overcame their fellows.
The inhabitants of the tropics have no such comforting reasons
for adoring the sinister forces which hem them in on every side.
For us, the notion 'river' implies (how obviously!) the notion
80 'bridge'. When we think of a plain, we think of agriculture,
towns, and good roads. The corollary of mountain is tunnel;
of swamp, an embankment; of distance, a railway. At latitude
zero, however, the obvious is not the same as with us. Rivers
imply wading, swimming, alligators. Plains mean swamps,
forests, fevers. Mountains are either dangerous or impassable.
To travel is to hack one's way laboriously through a tangled,
prickly, and venomous darkness. 'God made the country,' said
Cowper, in his rather too blank verse. In New Guinea he would

have had his doubts; he would have longed for the man-
90 made town.

B *In the first paragraph, the writer implies a number of ideas. Which
word or phrase (excluding proper names) conveys the implications
of the words in italics?*

89 Many people have accepted the divinity of nature *without
questioning the belief.* (One word)

19 *Not everyone* who shares this belief *has read any Wordsworth.*
(Three words)

75 *English* people claim to be spiritually refreshed by nature.
(Three words)

80 Men have in the past *sought out places of special sanctity.* (One
word)

7 Many English people seem to *enter into a special relationship
with natural scenery.* (One word)

60 'Good' *in line 3 means (choose one)*
virtuous, saintly, efficacious, efficient, sensible, compelling,
in fine condition, sound, splendid, pleasant

29 'Good' *in line 7 means (choose one)*
virtuous, saintly, efficacious, efficient, sensible, compelling,
in fine condition, sound, splendid, pleasant

C *The third paragraph*
Aldous Huxley finds that, for all its — **41** [wild/inexplicable/sheer/
initial/preliminary] *excitement, solitude ultimately* — **64** [is toler-
able/is an acquired taste/palls/ruins the tropics for the visitor/
imparts a thrill].

11 *The point about the* 'temperate sky' *(line 62) is that*
    (*a*) it makes us civilized people
    (*b*) it enables us to get about more
    (*c*) it results in milder forms of wild life
    (*d*) it encourages us to lead abstemious lives
    (*e*) it makes nature more beautiful

53 *The point about* 'Henry Ford' *(line 62) is that*
    (*a*) most families today own cars
    (*b*) the Americans have improved material conditions of life

(c) travel is easy in the twentieth century
(d) Ford is an inspiring example of business energy
(e) cars can convey us to magnificent views

37 *The worship of nature is, according to the writer*

(a) sentimental (b) harmless (c) comforting (d) blasphemous
(e) unrewarding

84 *Why is one's fear* 'salutary' *(line 67)?*

(a) the struggle is good for one's soul
(b) one is not tempted into complacency
(c) one greets nature as an enemy
(d) one's hostility serves nature right
(e) one becomes humble in the presence of nature

15 *Who or what are the* 'hosts of Nature' *(line 68)?*

(a) those who administer nature reserves
(b) the many species of animal life
(c) natural features of country that are hostile to man
(d) destructive weather conditions
(e) uncivilized tribes

47 'Their fellows' *(line 76) must be*

(a) primitive tribes that once inhabited England
(b) once wild areas now under human control
(c) creatures hostile to man
(d) the perils to health
(e) forests kept in a wild state but defined by boundaries

73 *Natural features are, in our eyes, things to*

(a) exploit for our own ends (b) admire (c) traverse and use
(d) destroy (e) disdain

1 . . . *but to those who live in the tropics the country is*

(a) a hostile environment
(b) uncomfortable for travellers
(c) something to be kept at bay
(d) a mixture of beauty and horror
(e) land hard to cultivate

43 *Huxley thinks Cowper's remark is*

(a) shallow (b) profound (c) inspiring (d) vague (e) idiotic

82 *In twentieth-century England, we seem to*

(*a*) endure (*b*) reverence (*c*) enslave (*d*) mock (*e*) overcome
nature . . .

26 *. . . but in fact we*

(*a*) fear (*b*) patronize (*c*) humour (*d*) use (*e*) ignore   *it*

56 *People in the tropics, on the other hand, regard it with*

(*a*) awe (*b*) apprehension (*c*) superciliousness (*d*) disfavour
(*e*) hatred

D *Consider the theories about man's relationship to his natural surroundings expressed by one or more of the following*

HENRY VAUGHAN, especially 'The Retreat', but elsewhere in
his poetry also.

GEORGE CRABBE, 'The Lover's Journey', from *Tales in Verse.*

WORDSWORTH, especially 'Lines composed a few miles from
Tintern Abbey', 'Resolution and Independence', *The Prelude,*
I and II.

TENNYSON, especially *In Memoriam,* LIV and LV.

EMILY BRONTË, *Wuthering Heights.*

WALTER BAGEHOT, 'The Ignorance of Man' from *Literary
Studies,* Dent (Everyman) 2 vols.; see also the *Pelican Book of
Victorian Prose,* Penguin.

GERARD MANLEY HOPKINS

GEORGE MEREDITH, especially 'The Woods of Westermain'
and *The Ordeal of Richard Feverel,* chapters 19 and 42.

THOMAS HARDY, the verse *passim,* and of the novels especially *The Woodlanders, The Return of the Native* and *Tess of the
D'Urbervilles.*

E. M. FORSTER, *A Passage to India,* E. Arnold, 1924; Penguin.

A. E. HOUSMAN

W. H. AUDEN, especially 'In Praise of Limestone' (in *Nones,*
Faber, 1952), and the 'Bucolics' (in *The Shield of Achilles,* Faber,
1948).

JOHN STEINBECK, *The Grapes of Wrath,* Heinemann, 1939.

WILLIAM FAULKNER, *passim,* see 'The Bear' from *Go Down,
Moses,* new edn., Chatto, 1960; Penguin.

R. S. THOMAS

II

† *No Further West*, by Dan Jacobson, 1957

On the foothills of the mountains were the houses of the rich, within easy reach of the suburban towns and the highways, yet set comfortably back from them. They were modern enough, these houses, many of them of bold and elaborate architecture, with split-levels and patios and carports and light timber beams exposed and flagged verandas outside glass doors that remained open through all the summer days and evenings. Yet somehow they did not seem attractive to live in, and I am still a little puzzled to know why; I think I would have preferred a house
10 in one of the suburban towns, if I had to live in California permanently, rather than those houses perched on the hill-tops or set against the flanks of the mountains.

In the towns, I suppose, one was able pretty much to forget about the seasons, about natural California altogether. This forgetfulness was helped by the fact that the seasons in California were not really noticeable: the sun shone most of the year, and while it was true that we had rain in the winter and none in the summer, there was no snow, no really bitter cold; when spring came the grass turned green and some of the trees put on a few
20 more leaves, and that was all; in summer the grass turned brown. These movements were all small; there was none of the slow and profound turning of the year that one has in other climates, and that penetrates the consciousness of even the most boxed-in city dweller in the blackest of cities. And then one's indifference to what lay beyond the highways and the drive-ins and the little wooden houses was encouraged too by the fact that so very often one could not see beyond them, anyway: hills and mountains and horizons were hidden often by the smog that came creeping down the Bay Area, walling it in, concentrating
30 the light upon what glittered and flickered near to hand. So sunk in the jumble, one was not reminded of the failure of the Californians to come to terms with the country that surrounded them. When the fog lifted, or when one was visiting one of these houses in the foothills, the reminder was always there.

It is difficult enough to talk about the relation of any people to the country that surrounds them; but in California the relationship which one felt seems even more difficult to describe than is usually the case. In South Africa, for instance, there is also a failure on the part of the country's inhabitants to come to terms
40 with the country in which they live. The cities are dwarfed by the spaces and silences that surround them; in Cape Town, in Kimberley, even in Johannesburg, one has just to lift one's head to become aware so often of the thinness and tenuousness of the relationship that the bold buildings and the telegraph poles have to the naked and indifferent veld around them. South Africans have just scratched the surface of their country, which remains always beyond them, unassailable, uninterpretable, always bigger and dryer and more imposing than they are or what they do to it. There is pathos in the relationship, a sense of loss and
50 powerlessness.

And England again is quite different. The people seem to fit the country (what is left of the country, outside the cities) and the country the people, so that one can hardly tell what is natural and what man-made. Each at its best over the centuries has become the other, in a congruence, a harmony of field and house, road and hedge, wood and village, moor and harbour, that is a continual surprise and reassurance to the spirit.

But in both South Africa and England there is this relationship, to be perceived and described. In California, however,
60 there seemed to be no congruence as in England; nor was there defeat and powerlessness, as in South Africa; powerlessness is the last thing one would ascribe to the Californians. Their towns and their houses are simply thrust down, ignoring, making null and unnoticeable the country on which they are built; and the country, for its part, seems to have nothing to do with the towns and the houses that have been placed on it. There is an abruptness in the change from what is man-made and what is natural, an equality of powers that has produced merely a disjuncture and an indifference.
70 And this too is new: that men should have been powerful enough to do this, to seem to ignore in this way the land they settle in.

E *Here is a summary of the second paragraph. Pick the appropriate words to fill each gap.*

In California, where hot weather — **78** [blazed/predominated/persisted/was common/lasted], — **86** [seasonable/seasonal/climatic/temporary/temporal] variations were so — **24** [slight/trivial/paltry/dull/indefinite] and — **46** [colourless/monotonous/obscure/rapid/superficial] as hardly to — **59** [irritate/impinge on/disconcert/embarrass/influence] the consciousness of town-dwellers. Moreover a — **6** [local/peculiar/sea/gleaming/protective] haze frequently — **54** [blurred/improved/blocked/adorned/beautified] the view of the surrounding countryside and — **69** [dazzled/diverted/restricted/assisted/blinded] one's vision to the — **20** [gay/fascinating/kaleidoscopic/impressive/garish] foreground of buildings that lined the motorways. On the rare occasions when one did see or enter the countryside, one realized how — **88** [faithless/impervious/unkind/off-hand/half-hearted] the Californians were to their — **33** [scene/scenery/resources/environment/advantages].

F *Reduce the rest of the passage to about 125 words.*

G *Both Huxley and Jacobson discuss the relationship between the English and their countryside. (We are not considering for the moment their comments on the tropics, South Africa or California.) Which of these ideas are found (a) in both, (b) in Aldous Huxley only, (c) in Dan Jacobson only, (d) in neither?*

63 The people dominate the country
4 The people and the country have often collaborated
49 The people ignore the country
71 The people indulge in sentimentality towards the country
18 The people travel confidently over the country
39 The people are afraid of the country
67 Much building has encroached on the country
14 The countryside has virtually been tamed

H *Produce your own local examples of the 'congruence' mentioned by Dan Jacobson, and also of 'incongruity'.*

I *How about the towns? How do you think the surroundings should be planned for a block of flats in a city? What sort of harmony between man and nature is possible in urban building? What should parks provide?*

J *Can you parallel the attitudes to their surroundings of the South Africans and the Californians as analysed by Dan Jacobson, either from your experience or your reading?*

K *The following may soon be extinct*
the rhinoceros, the polecat, the red squirrel, the lady's-slipper orchid, the clothes moth, the osprey.
On what grounds would you seek to preserve or destroy any of them?

L *What are the ultimate effects of the motor-car?*

Further reading

D. H. LAWRENCE, *Phoenix* (Posthumous Papers, ed. E. D. MacDonald), Heinemann, 1936 (Nottingham and the Mining Country).

R. S. R. FITTER, *Wild Life in Britain*, Penguin, 1963.

GAVIN MAXWELL, *Ring of Bright Water*, Longmans, 1960; Heritage of Literature Series.

T. H. WHITE, *The Goshawk*, Cape, 1951; Penguin; Longmans, Heritage of Literature Series

The New Naturalist Series, Collins.

III

'A Street in Cumberland', by Norman Nicholson (in *Rock Face*), 1948

The brick wall of the garden doubles
The long folds of the street;
Hydrangeas blow their blue-white bubbles
In plots of soil the size of carpets. Neat
Is the rough-cast, and the doors set back
Deep in the doorways, alternate numbers
Brassed on the boards above the lock –
And not a neighbour now remembers
That the eighth or ninth house from the end
Was not built with the street, but stood a farm
Two hundred years on its own land,
And the rest of the street was shunted firm
Against it when the town was made on the mosses.
Come round to the back and you will find

10

The old, uncovered walls – slate bosses
Two foot by two, with cobble-ducks for gable-end,
Cemented to a breccia that would stand
Square with its sandstone joints against the high
Blustering of the bragging wind
20   That skims the beard off the Irish Sea.
Where the cows bent to the stream,
And the sheep-dog looped the sheep,
The gutters drain the water. Yet a dream
Grips at the house when the roofs are asleep,
True to the loins of the rock that bred it. When the
    slag
Is puddled across the clouds, and curlews fly
Above the chimneys, the walls thrust like a crag
Through the dark tide of haematite in the night sky.

M *Here follows a short appreciation of this poem. Pick the appropriate word to fill each gap. Some of the questions are about the sense of the poem, but some also about the tone of the writer.*

This poem, by contrasting two types of architecture, also distinguishes the — **76** [development/quality/achievement/importance/ideals] of each life lived there. The brick wall, the doors set back and the locks suggest, for instance, — **28** [affluence/good taste/insulation/fear of burglars/homeliness]. The 'neat' rough-cast and the garden-plots 'the size of carpets' are made to seem — **91** [superficially ornamental/pretentious/attempts to score off the neighbours/the result of much toil/gaudy]; the hydrangeas that have been coaxed out of the mossy soil give an impression of — **52** [vulgarity/obtrusiveness/luxuriance/fragility/brilliance]. To be sure, the inhabitants lead — **22** [exciting/prosperous/healthy/orderly] lives, and give evidence of enjoying security and leisure; yet we are left with the impression that they are being encouraged to — **83** [agree/respond/assent/conform/return] to a suburban way of life; no house shows any individuality, and the feature that distinguishes one from another is stated to be merely its — **35** [garden/door/wall/flowers/number] – the detail that comes nearest to being — **79** [commonplace/disturbing/assertive/characteristic/pleasing].

What of the older building, which has been — **10** [destroyed by/superseded by/reconstructed as/absorbed into/overrun by] the new? And what of the older way of life, now — **51** [forgotten/ despised/a matter for pride/lamented/so out of date]? There was — **65** [little left of/no pretence about/little protection in/a historic interest in/something unusual about] these walls – they were 'uncovered' – so that it is now possible actually to see the — **25** [bricks/craftsmanship/ingenuity/architecture/subtlety] with which the builders assembled their various local stones so as to keep out rough weather. The inhabitants of the buildings must have struggled all their lives in an attempt to — **72** [farm/ make do with/drain/enrich/beautify] this unpromising soil in this menacing climate. As he describes the prevailing wind, the poet conveys to us the — **40** [poetic nature/simplicity/vigorous humour/grimness/uneducated character] of the language once spoken in this part of Cumberland. Even today, seen against a turbulent night sky, the house looks more like — **57** [an excrescence/a monstrosity/a home/a local building/an outcrop] than an artificial structure. In the same way, the inhabitants must once have — **2** [belonged to/loved/quarried/improved/despaired of] their natural surroundings more — **44** [crudely/ happily/rapidly/intimately/suitably] than those who now inhabit it.

N *Describe in prose or verse another juxtaposition of old and new (e.g. the modern railway station at Rome, which incorporates a short stretch of ancient Roman wall. But you need not describe buildings).*

O *What two hints of industrial development are there in the poem? What is the implication?*

P *What in your opinion is the most striking feature of the poem which has been omitted from the appreciation written above?*

Q *What comparison in subject-matter occurs to you between this poem and the passages of Aldous Huxley and Dan Jacobson?*

R *Write an essay* In Praise of Suburbia *or on* Cities of the Future.

12 Intelligence :
Education : Equality

I

† *Know your own I.Q.*, by H. J. Eysenck, 1962

The question is often raised whether intelligence is innate or
acquired; this is often referred to as the nature-nurture controversy. Before closing this account of I.Q. tests a few words
may perhaps be said about this thorny problem. To begin with,
then, it is clear that children tend to resemble their parents with
regard to their I.Q.; indeed, until the child is six years of age or
thereabouts a better prediction of his future I.Q. is obtained
by measuring that of his parents than by measuring his own!
However, this fact does not help us very much, as this similarity
10 could clearly be due either to hereditary or environmental
factors; the child could resemble his parents because he inherited the genes making for intelligent behaviour, or he could
resemble them because he grew up in an environment largely
reflecting their intelligence. Actually our main information
regarding inheritance of intelligence comes rather from the fact
that while children largely do resemble their parents, there are
systematic deviations which can only be accounted for in terms
of hereditary causes. The phenomenon I have in mind is usually
called *regression*, and it was first observed in relation to height,
20 which is known to be very much an inherited characteristic, at
least in countries with an adequate food supply. It was found
that the children of very tall parents are taller than the average,
but not as tall as their parents; similarly, for small parents,
their children are smaller than the average, but taller than their
parents. On both sides children appear to *regress* to the average,

81

and it is quite simple to account for this fact in terms of the Mendelian theory of heredity. Now exactly the same phenomenon has been observed in relation to intelligence, and if the reader will turn back to a previous table which gives the I.Q.s of groups of parents in various social strata, and of children whose parents come from the same social strata, he will see the degree of regression involved, which is almost identical with that found in studies of height. Our main evidence for the importance of heredity therefore comes not from the similarities observed between parents and children but from the discovery of systematic differences between them which find an easy explanation in hereditary terms but which are very difficult to account for along environmental lines.

The second type of proof frequently advanced relates to the study of identical and fraternal twins. Identical twins completely share their heredity while fraternal twins are no more alike than ordinary siblings, i.e. share heredity only to the extent of about 50 per cent. It will be clear that if environment has a strong effect, then identical twins should be no more alike than should fraternal twins, whereas if heredity is a stronger force, then identical twins should be much more alike than fraternal twins. Many studies have dealt with twins brought up together, and the universal findings have been that identical twins are very much more alike. Rather small-scale studies in the United States, and a recent rather more extensive study in Great Britain, have shown that when you take twins, separated early in life and brought up under different conditions, there nevertheless remains a definite tendency for the identical ones to be more alike than the fraternal ones. This method of investigation also strongly favours the hereditary rather than the environmentalistic point of view.

As a third proof you may perhaps look at breeding studies done with animals. Here a test of ability suitable for the animal in question is constructed, and a group of animals is tested. High scorers are then interbred to produce a bright strain and low-scoring animals are interbred to produce a dull strain. The animals in each successive generation are tested, and the brightest and dullest ones respectively are picked out and interbred again. After a dozen or so generations it is found that there is practically no overlap in performance between the bright

and the dull strains, all the bright offspring doing better on the test than any of the dull. The weight we would place on this evidence depends of course on whether we view intelligence as a biological characteristic which is not necessarily confined to
70 humans but can also be assessed, although at a rather lower level, in other mammals. It is perhaps in conjunction with the other proofs already advanced that this one assumes particular importance.

A fourth proof is in a sense the obverse of the one in which identical twins were used. In the twin experiments we keep heredity identical and let the environment vary; clearly we can attempt instead to keep the environment constant and let heredity vary. This is done by studying orphanage children sent there shortly after birth. The whole life of these children is spent
80 in an environment which is practically identical for all the children; if environment determines intelligence, then all the children should have very similar I.Q.s to each other. Only heredity could produce differences in I.Q. between the children. When this experiment was done, it was found that intelligence in orphanage children showed practically the same degree of variability as intelligence in normal children subject to great differences in environmental conditions; here again therefore heredity appears as the prime factor in the determination of individual differences in intelligence.

90 Many other types of tests and types of experimental design have been tried, but those mentioned above are the most conclusive ones, and they are not contradicted by any other evidence. They indicate quite clearly the importance of heredity, and it is possible to define a rough and ready numerical estimate for the relative contribution of heredity and environment in Western countries at the present time. It appears that about 80 per cent of all the factors contributing to individual differences of intelligence are hereditary, 20 per cent environmental; in other words, heredity is four times as important as
100 environment.

It should be noted that these figures are rough averages only, and that they only apply to the Western world at the present time. They have no absolute value, since they depend entirely on the social and educational practices in a given country. Where there is universal free education for all children, and

possibly universal free access to university education as well, then obviously hereditary factors are most free to manifest themselves. In countries where there is education only for a privileged few, the potential intelligence of the others may be
110 repressed to a considerable degree. We cannot therefore extrapolate the '80 per cent–20 per cent' figure to apply to this country one hundred years ago, or to Iran at the present time, to take but two examples, nor can we extrapolate them into the future; it is quite possible that in fifty years' time the relative contribution of heredity to the results of intelligence tests will be even higher than it is now, provided the trend towards greater equality in education continues.

A *Eysenck's first proof could be summarized as follows*
Children of — **26** parents have been shown to be, on average, less — **44** than their — **35**. This is what one would expect from reading — **7**, and there is no doubt that — **28** causes this — **68** (to give it its technical name). We find exactly the same — **13** when we consider — **62**, and we therefore conclude that here too — **16** is the important factor, rather than — **30**.
   What is the right word for each numbered gap?

B *Summarize, in about 50 words, the third proof.*

C *Here are seven groups mentioned in the second and fourth proofs*
   (*a*) identical twins brought up together
   (*b*) identical twins brought up apart
   (*c*) fraternal twins brought up together
   (*d*) fraternal twins brought up apart
   (*e*) ordinary siblings brought up together or apart
   (*f*)   unrelated children brought up together
   (*g*) unrelated children brought up apart
   Which group (give the letter) fits each numbered gap in the following statements?

—49	have 50% shared heredity,	0% shared environment		
— 2	„ 100% „	„ 100% „	„	„
—39	„ 0% „	„ 100% „	„	„
—59	„ 100% „	„ 0% „	„	„

84

—**22** have 0% shared heredity, 0% shared environment

—**66**   „   50%   „   „   100%   „   „

Many studies show that — **42** are more alike in I.Q. than — **14**.
Some studies show that — **52** are more alike in I.Q. than — **19**.
It has been shown that — **47** are very little more alike in I.Q
than — **64**.

D *In the last paragraph*

11 which clause describes the present situation in the Western
world?

71 which clause describes the present situation in Iran?

40 Do you suppose that in England, in 1862, the hereditary
factor in intelligence was more than 80 per cent, about 80
per cent, or less than 80 per cent?

II

† *Education for To-morrow*, by John Vaizey, 1962

Are we not at the present moment educating the most intelligent at the expense of the less able, who need more attention,
better conditions, and greater help just because their environment impedes their chances of expressing themselves, of
acquiring new skills, and of understanding the society in which
they live? Why are we doing this, and how did it come about?

We know that not everyone in our society is getting the best
possible education to meet his needs and to develop his abilities,
and yet selection is said at present to be made on the basis of
10 intelligence. But to-day we know far more about ability and
intelligence than we did. So much more, in fact, that it is now
clear that the great tradition of belief in equality of opportunity was not only correct – in that there were still great
reserves of untapped ability in our society – but that it was
even an understatement of what needs to be achieved if all
sorts and kinds of abilities are to be developed to the full.

One of the great drives towards improvement in education

has always come from the passionate concern of reformers with equality. Until recently this was defined simply as equality of
20 opportunity – that, given the opening, those with intelligence would rise to the top. It was believed that there were many working-class girls and boys – village Hampdens – who, if offered the chance, could become great statesmen, great scientists, or great writers. One or two in a thousand could be identified and rescued – the rest would be left. Scholarships were created to provide places for children of high ability, largely from the white-collar working class. Gradually, with the growth of sophistication in genetic ideas and techniques for measuring ability, it became clear that a great deal of talent of the
30 highest level was, in fact, lost by inegalitarian systems of education. The idea that equality of opportunity might mean opportunity to develop any abilities a child might have, even if these did not lie solely in the intellectual field, is a much more modern interpretation of this phrase. It is only recently that it has become accepted that every child is entitled to an adequate education, though at the present moment only the top five per cent of the intelligence distribution gain an education which is in any respect equivalent to that specially provided for middle-class children by their parents.

40 Yet in principle and in law every child now has the right to an education suited to his age, abilities, and aptitude, and a great deal of the effort of educational psychologists is concerned with placing children in schools or on courses which appear suited to their talents. However, the work of educational psychologists is now suspect to egalitarians; the job of the psychologists has seemed to be to pick the winners in the race to the top rather than to help those they discard to widen their horizons. Their thinking seems to have been based upon the assumption that it was possible to make a selection of children at a com-
50 paratively early age, which could later be justified by the achievements of these children. The more competent and distinguished scientists in this field have long known that most of these predictions were self-confirming. That is to say, a child from a good home sent to a good school was bound to seem more intelligent, to have the chance to be better educated, and to get farther ahead than a child from a poor home sent to an overcrowded elementary school. In addition, recent

86

inquiries suggest that intelligence, in so far as it can be measured at all, is largely acquired. Marxist scholars have all along held 60 that intelligence is entirely acquired, but Western scholars argue against this theory from their research on the similar achievements of identical twins separated at birth, and the different achievements of non-identical twins brought up together. Similar cases have suggested that there must be an inherent quality in intelligence, even if the acquired element is a large part of the whole. Nevertheless, those systems of education which, like the Russian, are based upon the assumption that all children are born equal, are probably more satisfactory in practice than those like our own, which are based on the 70 assumption that children are born intellectually sheep or goats.

A great deal of the debate about equality has now become out of date, since it is based upon three assumptions, none of which is any longer believed to be correct. The first is that educational resources will always be scarce, so that a choice must be made between the children of any age group who should be adequately educated, and those who should receive second best. Since our society is now entering a period of great wealth, and already has the capacity to provide an education system which is satisfactory for any child, there is no need to 80 maintain this assumption of scarcity.

Secondly, it has always been assumed that society depended upon the identification of some exceptional people who would later become the leaders, while the great mass would be doing routine and humdrum jobs well within the capabilities of anybody with a minimum of intelligence and training.

This is now emphatically not the case. In a modern economy jobs present a wide range of demands on talent and ability, and a highly productive society makes enormous demands upon people of all abilities, both on their general level of competence 90 in such matters as reading, writing, calculating, driving, or managing technical equipment, and on their ability to meet the requirements of an increasingly complex social organization, while at the same time it requires a high level of emotional adjustment to situations of rapid change. Learning these techniques, abilities and basic emotional adjustments depends to an increasing extent upon the educational system. It is becoming more important to educate the people of average and less than average ability than it is to educate the highly able. In any case, study after study has shown that unless a very wide range of 100 ability is educated, some very able people are inevitably going to fall through the net. Even in a society such as ours, which has been organized for nearly fifty years on a basis of some equality of opportunity, two-fifths of the top ten per cent of the ability distribution still left school at fifteen in recent years.

The third assumption which is no longer true is that ability is a fixed quantum which can be identified and which to all intents and purposes remains constant throughout life. It has now been shown that the average level of ability has risen rather than fallen, if measured in terms of what the average 110 person can do. It has been shown that children brought up in homes with satisfactory emotional adjustment, sent to good schools, staying on at school until the latest possible date, and then taking up interesting work, become more intelligent in every sense than those to whom this does not happen. In so far as there is a rise in the standard of living of the average home, an improvement in the average school, and a lengthening of school life, the number of able people will therefore multiply.

This new knowledge makes it necessary to re-examine the whole concept of 'equality of opportunity'. Mr. Anthony Cros-120 land has recently drawn a vital distinction between the 'weak' and the 'strong' definition of equal opportunity. The weak definition (which has always been accepted as the only definition up to now) is that all children of equal (measured) ability should have roughly the same start in life. The strong definition takes account of recent psychological knowledge, which points out that ability is largely acquired, and that a child can become more or less intelligent according to the kind of family he has and the social and educational experience he receives. It asserts that, subject to differences in heredity and infantile 130 experience, every child should have the same opportunity for acquiring measured intelligence, in so far as this can be controlled by social action.

This is clearly a revolutionary principle. It means a rapid shift towards creating a society where every child has a good home, which in turn means, as an integral part of the educational process, eliminating low incomes, bad housing, and badly-educated parents. It means sending every child to a good

school till he is at least seventeen, and as far as possible eliminating any final decisions before that age as to his future
140 education and job, in order not to narrow his academic field
too early. In practice it would suggest, for example, that if
boarding schools have anything to give (which I doubt, except
for a tiny minority) it should be given to the culturally deprived
and not to the well-endowed.

E

31 *How many of the following assumptions (and which ones) are
essential to the argument of the first paragraph but are not explicitly
stated in that paragraph?*

(a) more education for some means less for others

(b) slow-witted children are more teachable than bright
children

(c) intelligent children are comparatively quick at understanding the society in which they live

(d) the less able have to pay fees so that the intelligent can
be educated

(e) poor environment handicaps children in their attempts
to acquire new skills

(f) less able children have a poor environment

56 *Those who favoured equality of opportunity are said in the second
paragraph to have been right*

(a) on moral grounds

(b) on grounds of expediency

(c) on egalitarian grounds

(d) on logical grounds

(e) because they understated the truth

23 *In the second paragraph the words 'abilities' and 'intelligence'
are both used because*

(a) they are quite different

(b) they are exactly the same, but the author did not want
to repeat one word too often

(c) 'intelligence' is the wider word, and includes 'abilities'

(d) 'abilities' is the wider word, and includes 'intelligence'

(e) the two words together are complementary

69 *The working-class children are called* 'village Hampdens' *(line 22) because*

(a) they would become great
(b) they were one or two in a thousand
(c) they could withstand tyranny
(d) their great qualities were hidden
(e) they were well known to others in a small village

53 *The rest would be left (line 25)*

(a) in the village
(b) outside school altogether
(c) without having had an equal opportunity
(d) in danger
(e) in the working-class

33 'An adequate education' *(line 35) must in this context mean*

(a) an education similar to that which a scholarship gains for a child
(b) an education that fully develops whatever ability a child has
(c) a middle-class education
(d) an education that takes a child to the top
(e) an education that is the same for all children

25 *Are* 'middle-class children' *(line 38) referred to here as being*

(a) in grammar schools
(b) those who benefit from the theory of 'equality of opportunity'
(c) in fee-paying schools
(d) educated at home
(e) helped by scholarships?

63 *Are* 'those they discard' *(line 47)*

(a) working-class children
(b) less intelligent children
(c) slow runners
(d) children who have refused help from educational psychologists
(e) children who are not placed in schools at all?

F *Express in your own words the two criticisms which the writer makes of the work of educational psychologists.*

G *Summarize in your own words the three assumptions and the writer's contention that each is now untrue (lines 71–117). Write your own comments on whichever one of these contentions seems to you the least satisfactory.*

H *Write a debate between parent, child, schoolmaster, and taxpayer on the suggestions made in the final paragraph.*

I 'It means sending every child to a good school till he is at least seventeen, and as far as possible eliminating any final decisions before that age as to his future education and job.' *(line 137) Describe what the last two years should be like in a good school intended for those who at present leave school at fifteen.*

J *In your own words present the case for educating children of average (or below average) ability more effectively than we do now.*

K 'Mr Vaizey's whole thesis is muddled, sentimental, impracticable and unrealistic.' *Discuss.*

III

† *Repair the Ruins*, by Harry Blamires, 1950

It is essential, therefore, to clear our minds on the subject of equality before we theorise further about the purpose of education.

First of all, equality just does not belong to the world of intellectual attainment. The very function of education is to increase innate inequalities. John Smith has an exceptionally high intelligence, and James Brown has an exceptionally low one. At the age of six months there will be little to choose between them. If there is any sense in education at all, there will
10 be increasingly more and more difference between Smith and Brown in intellectual depth and range as they proceed through primary school, secondary school and (in one case) university. This is not to say that the best possible should not be done for Brown; but that best will surely be (in terms of intellect) a little

thing compared to the endowment that a centuries-old tradition of learning and culture has to offer Smith.

As everyone knows, equality, in the educational world, means equality of opportunity, and nothing more. Suppose we build up our conception of the ideal educational system honestly and
20 logically on this basis. It means that the poorest boy in the meanest slum should have the opportunity to get the best academic education in the land, however costly, if his capacities warrant it. To give substance to this conception, the educational system would have to expand *qualitatively* rather than *quantitatively*. Free schools, giving an education comparable to that provided by the best Public Schools, would testify to real equality of opportunity. Before the war there was considerable development in this direction. Some municipal grammar schools advanced to the stage at which their pupils could com-
30 pete successfully with Public School boys in open scholarship examinations. The logical next move was to take the best of these state grammar schools and lift standards higher still by better staffing and more selective entry. This would have been a qualitative expansion of the state educational system based soundly on the theory of equal opportunity for all.

Instead of this, one kind of educational advance – and the advance of true social equality – has been frustrated (temporarily, we hope) by the advent of a shallow and ill-considered phrase, 'Parity of Esteem'. The theory is that John Smith must
40 not be considered superior to James Brown because he has got a grammar-school scholarship, whilst Brown is plodding on at the secondary modern school. Let us analyse this idea. First, Smith *is* superior to Brown intellectually. As a candidate for academic education, he is superior. As a brain, he is superior. He got the grammar-school scholarship because he is superior, or else our educational system is topsy-turvy indeed.

Very well, then, what does 'parity of esteem' really mean? It means that there must be no snobbery; no pride on the part of Smith and his family, no contempt of Brown. In short, this
50 is a moral question, pure and simple. The demand is for an attack upon pride and for the nourishment of true humility. If humility is in vogue, then no problem arises; for Smith and Smith's parents respect Brown as a fellow human being and recognise that innate intellectual inequalities are but by the

grace of God. And whoever heard of a moral question solved by administration and organisation? You can plan and scheme till the day of doom, adjust scales of pay, equalise holidays and improve buildings, but you will not lay so much as a finger-weight of influence upon the moral nature of man. 'Parity of
60 esteem' between grammar and non-grammar schools is a dream and a mockery; and we must beware lest it serve for a cloak over the most powerful assault upon real equality of opportunity that England has seen since secondary education began.

The state committed itself years ago to a quantitative expansion of education, and now it has put the brake on such qualitative expansion as was arising from the efforts and idealism of earnest teachers in grammar schools. Let us try to get a bird's-eye view of the development which has brought us to the present state of affairs. When state secondary education began, it
70 naturally drew its pattern and inspiration from the traditions embodied in the Public Schools and endowed grammar schools. This pattern was based upon an aristocratic conception of education. The pupils were to be introduced to the world of thought and culture, and the best of them were to be prepared for the universities. Humane studies formed the core of the curriculum. Of course state secondary schools multiplied rapidly, and it was a watered-down version of the traditional humane curriculum which found its way into most of them. Nevertheless, the predominance of the study of languages (including Latin),
80 History, Divinity, English Literature and Mathematics, showed the allegiance of the curriculum to the traditional ideal of humane culture; and it was inevitable that this should be so, if only for the reason that there was no other ideal to serve as an inspiration.

As time went on the diluted version of the humane curriculum was stamped into a very recognisable shape by the School Certificate Examination proclaiming its attachment to the traditional ideal by its connection with university matriculation. Thus thousands and thousands of boys and girls were turned
90 out annually with the minimum academic equipment demanded by the universities as a starting-point for advanced study. These young people had a smattering of Latin and of French; they had mechanically swotted up the facts of a limited period of political history, they had wearily 'got up' a few treasures of literature,

memorising lines for quotation and training themselves at the jig-saw game of context identification. We know how little it all meant in so many cases; and now we are striving to get rid of it. But *why* did the scheme of educating all men to the old humane pattern fail?

100 It failed because only a fraction – a very small fraction – of the human race is equipped by taste, temperament and talent to pursue the course, I will not say to its logical conclusion, but to the stage at which it begins to have meaning. And the course *has* a meaning eventually; when you have progressed from Greek and Latin Accidence to the study of Plato, Aristotle, Cicero and Livy; or when you have progressed from the politics of Queen Victoria's reign to an intelligent interest in the history of our civilisation. The scheme failed, then, because precious few of mankind have the capacity to comprehend a 110 meaning in history, to arrive at a philosophical view of human life, to appreciate the splendours of artistic achievement, to understand the birth, growth and significance of civilisations, cultures and systems of thought.

We are naive if this discovery surprises us, and we are positively stupid if it horrifies us. What would become of a world populated entirely by philosophers, artists, connoisseurs and men of letters? The attempt to educate all men to the old aristocratic pattern was doomed to failure from the start; and if it had been doomed to success, it would have destroyed our 120 civilisation. We have wakened up to this fact, though we do not all express our opinions as honestly as we might. And because, as we think, we have wakened up to realities, a new and menacing danger has arisen. Instead of admitting: 'This that we call education is not for all men, not even for the majority of men: when we present it neat, most of them cannot take it; and when we water it down, it does not appear to do them much good: we must reserve it only for those fitted for it, making sure that everyone has the *chance* to get it' – instead of this, we are now saying: 'This that has been called education for several hun-130 dreds of years is not in fact education at all, for it suits only a few of England's millions: we must abolish it and replace it by real education which suits the needs and capacities of all.'

It is a crazy remedy for a crazy situation. Our first concern in the handling of the nation's educational system should be to

make sure that the positive achievements of the past are not negatived by empty-headed reformers. I have shown already how all thought and all culture are an inheritance from the past. Education has the task of leading us to share all that dwells in the recollected consciousness of centuries – an inheritance past
140 the size of dreaming. It is not primarily the duty of education to lead explorers in search of unknown and uncharted lands. The kingdoms of thought and the kingdoms of man's ear and eye, already exist, established and secure. Education has for centuries been leading men into these kingdoms: the gates are open and the ways are well-trodden. If we wander off in new directions, we shall discover that we no longer have intelligible contact with the past: and yet the treasure we seek is itself contained in the past. Education is the most traditional thing under the sun. The humane educational curriculum can never, of course,
150 be in danger from the educated; but, like all education, it is, and will be, menaced by many of those who have learned to read and write. It is the business of our ancient Public Schools, our grammar schools and our universities to defend it. It is the business of the state to make it accessible to all. Only a few will be of the right tastes, temperament and talent to make use of it. But if social democracy means anything at all, it means that selection for the traditional academic education will not be determined by financial means or social status, but will be dependent upon aptitude and ability.

L *Find the most appropriate words (twelve out of the twenty given below) to fill the gaps in this summary of the second paragraph.*

Education, by its very — **67**, militates against — **43**; for its — **4** is increasingly to add — **60** of — **36** to that — **60** of — **50** which exists when education begins. Even though the best possible — **20** be made for the boy who has little — **46** for intellectual — **9**, the able boy must still enter on a far richer — **55**, since it is — **38** that give — **70** to it.

access, aptitude, attainment, brains, constitution, disparity, equality, function, help, hope, inheritance, intelligence, intensity, love, nature, provision, similarity, studies, stupidity, teaching

95

M *You are asked to give a three-minute talk in Hyde Park, commending the proposals made in the third paragraph – and justifying them as 'true social equality'. Words like 'conception', 'testify', and 'qualitatively' would lose the attention of your audience; yet you must present the whole of Blamires's argument. Write down what you would say.*

N 'John Smith must not be considered superior to James Brown.' *Are you satisfied with Blamires's argument that this 'parity of esteem' cannot be achieved by the State's actions? If not, refute it.*

  Yet two sentences [**17** *which two?*] *reveal that the theory should rather be represented by the sentence –* 'Barchester Grammar School must not be considered superior to Barchester Secondary Modern School'. *Does this affect Blamires's arguments? Attack or defend the idea of* 'parity of esteem' *as between one school and another.*

O *Write a précis of the next three paragraphs (lines 64–113) in about 100 words.*

P *Describe in your own words what the* 'crazy remedy' *(line 133) consists of.*

Q 'All thought and all culture are an inheritance from the past.' *Discuss.*

R *List the points 1. of similarity, 2. of difference, between the Blamires extract and this letter to* The Times *(1963).*

Sir,

  Sorry though we may be for the deflated egos of the B-stream, there is no 'disguising' the fact that some children are As, some Bs, and some XYZs. Every sheep will know he is not a goat, whether he is branded or not. Children are not as easily deceived concerning their abilities as are their parents. As for the 'snobbery' involved, if they are not allowed to feel superior about their intellects they will inevitably find other and worse things to feel superior about, such as the length of their hair or the colour of their skins.

  Of greater importance is the problem, so unfashionable as to be almost unmentionable, of those forgotten few, the extra-bright children; the Super As. It is on these that the future of the nation largely depends, yet all too often their talents are allowed to atrophy in an unstreamed class. To be an adventurous mountain goat in a class of 39 sheep is to suffer agonies of boredom, frustration, and sometimes ostracism. Since children are adaptable by nature they soon learn to conform, realizing that any attempt to outshine the others is not praised but is regarded as unfair, if not un-English. Our tradition (surely a recent one?) of doing just enough to get by and never playing to win thus begins in infancy and continues into the adult world of work and entertainment, with its strikes, anti-heroes, and immature delinquent idols.

I submit, Sir, that the spirit of 'unfair competition' of which your correspondent complains (May 16) is exactly what is needed in our schools to-day: a revival of that spirit of emulation and endeavour which alone can save us from becoming a nation of sheep.

S *Write a spirited reply to this letter.*

T *Write an essay entitled* Quality is more important than equality.

U 'Mr Blamires has written a reactionary and snobbish attack on the average child.' *Discuss.*

V *Which of these three writers is*
  (*a*) the least emotional
  (*b*) the least logical
  (*c*) the least concerned about equality
  (*d*) the least elegant writer of prose?

W *List the points of disagreement*
  1. between Eysenck and Vaizey on 'Intelligence'
  2. between Vaizey and Blamires on 'Educational Opportunity'.

X '*Le style, c'est l'homme.*' *Describe the character of one of these three writers, with illustrations both from what he says and from the way in which he says it.*

Y *Write, for* The Times *of 1 January 1985, a 1,500 word article entitled* English Education: the last twenty years.

13 The Language of Science

I

† *Philosophy and the Physicists*, by Susan Stebbing, 1937

In these days of popular expositions, both written and broadcast, of Outlines, and of mammoth Guides to the Intelligent
Man – guides through science, guides through economics,
guides through philosophy, guides through chaos – the common
reader cannot be unaware that the sciences in general and the
physical sciences in particular have been developing rapidly and
that in the course of this development certain changes, des-
cribable as 'revolutionary', have occurred. These developments in science have a twofold interest. First, their results have
10 given us information, often surprising, about the world we live
in. Secondly, the following out of scientific method is in itself
exciting, affording us the purest of all satisfactions – intellectual satisfaction. There is among common readers a genuine
interest in scientific research, a desire to follow as far as a layman can what is being found and to understand the implications of these findings. Some of us are prepared to attempt to
make the considerable intellectual effort required in order to
understand even a non-technical exposition of recent developments in physics. The writing of such an exposition is un-
20 doubtedly difficult. It requires not only great powers of exposition but also an apprehension of the sort of difficulties the layman is likely to find and the skill to surmount them. We can
hardly complain if these matters are not made entirely clear to
us. Nevertheless, there are not a few scientists who have written
books that to some extent satisfy our needs. Unfortunately,

however, there are other famous scientists who do not seem to realize that their subject has an intrinsic interest for the common reader, and accordingly they seek to arouse his emotions, thereby inducing a frame of mind inimical to intellectual dis-
30 cernment. Popularizations of such a kind constitute a grave danger to thinking clearly. Possibly the authors themselves are at times wrought up to a pitch of emotional excitement, unduly impressed by the strangeness of their discoveries. I say '*unduly impressed*' because, however strange may be the accounts of recent physical speculations, these physical speculations are themselves the development of the normal procedure of scientific method. The invention of new and more delicate scientific instruments has extended the physicist's range of experience; fresh mathematical techniques have had to be devised to deal
40 with the discoveries thus made. It must not, however, be too hastily assumed that these new instruments and these new mathematical devices constitute in themselves a radical transformation of the nature of our knowledge. Some of our scientific guides, writing in moments of emotional exaltation, have found it easier to mystify the common reader than to enlighten him.

A

72 *What is the writer's attitude to* 'popular expositions'? *Quote phrases to justify your answer.*

1 *This passage forms one long paragraph. At which point could it conveniently be split into two paragraphs? Summarize the topic of each of the two paragraphs now formed and write out the two topic sentences.*

58 *Against each of the following statements put either √ √ or √ or ? or ×. Put √ √ if it is stated as a principal idea, √ if it is a subsidiary idea, ? if it is not expressed in the passage, and × if it is positively denied.*

(*a*) There is a glut of popular expositions on the market
(*b*) The common reader feels it his duty to keep abreast of ideas in modern physics
(*c*) The common reader, before tackling modern physics, needs to have his emotions aroused
(*d*) The common reader, in approaching modern physics, requires assistance from sympathetic experts

(e) Many laymen want to learn as much about modern
     physics as is within their capacity
(f) Modern physics offers the common reader a mental
     challenge
(g) The latest discoveries in physics should make us view
     the subject in an entirely new light
(h) Some popularizing scientists have made physics obscure
     to us because their expositions are so dry
(i) Some popularizing scientists have written with a fervour
     not in keeping with their subjects
(j) Some popularizing scientists have deliberately mystified
     their readers

15 *Write down three qualities which the writer thinks necessary for a
   specialist who expounds his subject to laymen. Are there any other
   obvious qualities?*

II

† An article by J. W. N. Watkins, printed in *The Listener*, 18 April 1963

Some time ago I was at a lecture by an eminent biologist. His
aim was to throw light on the nature of scientific discovery by
examining three discoveries in his own field, the third being one
he had made himself. What struck me was that in each case
there was considerable divergence between what had actually
happened and the published account of the discovery. When
he came to his own discovery, the lecturer gave a short and
rather baffling summary of it, remarking that this was how he
had written it up at the time, and that he would now explain
10 what had really happened. What he now said was not only more
interesting, it was much more easily understood. Afterwards I
asked him why he had not published the fuller and more reveal-
ing version. He hesitated and then said that he supposed he had
felt that he should confine himself to what could be checked by
repeatable experiments. I believe that this conscientious feeling

which constrained him to report his discovery in a censored way that would hardly be understood except by his co-specialists, has a philosophical ancestry, which I will now investigate.

One of the objections made against Descartes' *Méditations*
20 was that he ought to have propounded his arguments in geometrical fashion. Descartes' reply was so interesting and important that I will quote it at length. He distinguished between two methods of exposition, his own method of analysis and the geometrical method of synthesis, and he said:

'Analysis shows the true way by which a thing was methodically discovered . . . so that, if the reader care to follow it and give sufficient attention to everything, he understands the matter no less perfectly and makes it as much his own *as if he had discovered it himself. . . .*

30 'Synthesis contrariwise employs an opposite procedure. . . . It does indeed clearly demonstrate its conclusions, and it employs a long series of definitions, postulates, axioms, theorems. . . . The reader, however hostile and obstinate, is compelled to render his assent. Yet this method is not so satisfactory as the other and does not equally well content the eager learner, because *it does not show the way in which the matter taught was discovered. . . .*

'I have used in my Meditations only analysis, which is the best and truest method.'

Paraphrasing Descartes, we may say that one method is to
40 take the reader into your confidence by explaining to him how you arrived at your discovery; the other is to bully him into accepting a conclusion by parading a series of propositions which he must accept and which lead to it. The first method allows the reader to re-think your own thoughts in their natural order. It is an autobiographical style. Writing in this style you include, not what you had for breakfast on the day of discovery, but any significant consideration which helped you to arrive at your idea. In particular, you say what your aim was – what problems you were trying to solve and what you hoped
50 from a solution of them. The other style suppresses all this. It is didactic and intimidating.

Descartes' description of the latter, synthetic method of exposition can be generalized to cover a way of expounding so-called 'inductive' material as well as deductive systems like Euclidean geometry. The Euclidean ideal was to prove theo-

rems by deducing them from self-evident axioms. The inductive
ideal was to verify laws by inducing them from the results of
repeatable experiments. Thus the inductive version of the synthetic method would consist in first stating the results of a series
60 of experiments and then drawing a seemingly inescapable
general conclusion from them. This is the essence of what Popper calls the inductive style. Someone writing in this style may,
of course, go on to employ inductively established – or allegedly
established – 'laws' as axioms and then proceed in a Euclidean
manner (as Heinrich Hertz did in his *The Principles of Mechanics
Presented in a New Form*). My general name for all styles of scientific exposition, which instead of taking the reader into the writer's
confidence with a piece of candid intellectual autobiography,
aim at an impersonal rehearsal of justifications for a scientific
70 'finding' is, *didactic dead-pan*: 'didactic' because the intention is
to teach or convince the reader rather than to excite his interest,
and 'dead-pan' because this is usually done in the flat, auth-
oritative tone in which manufacturers' handbooks are written.

A good deal of unnecessary incomprehension is created by
the widespread use of a didactic dead-pan style both by scientists and by non-scientists wishing to sound scientific. Why has
it been so generally adopted? Descartes, we know, was against
it, and Descartes' autobiographical style was a model of lucid-
ity. Why was not *it* generally adopted?
80 After Descartes came 'the incomparable Mr. Newton'; and
Newton expounded his system in a magisterial manner. The
first edition of his *Principia*, after a short and unrevealing preface, begins with eight definitions and three axioms. Or take the
opening sentence of his *Opticks*:

> My design in this Book is not to explain the properties of Light
> by Hypotheses, but to propose and prove them by Reason and
> Experiments: in order to which I shall premise the following
> Definitions and Axioms.

Eight definitions and eight axioms follow. Notice the mixture
90 of modesty and assurance. We are not to suppose that, in an
attempt to solve important problems, that ingenious man Isaac
Newton has worked out some interesting and fruitful hypotheses. We are presented with findings established by Reason
and Experiment – two happily married deities whose faithful
amanuensis Newton is. Actually, of course, it was Newton's

fallible ideas that Newton presented. Some of them turned out quite soon to be false. Cartesian physics was defeated by Newtonian physics; and it was Newton's style of exposition, rather than Descartes', which tended to be imitated. My friend 100 Joseph Agassi believes that Newton adopted the magisterial style deliberately as part of his critic-silencing strategy. Also there was a philosophical idea which, in one guise or another, was generally held in Newton's time and which surely helped to encourage didactic dead-pan. Essentially, this idea is simple. It is this: knowledge has an extra-human source, erroneous opinion has a human source. To put this idea another way: true ideas about nature are somehow instilled into us by nature, false ideas are manufactured by us. Knowledge has an objective source, error starts up subjectively. Knowledge is impersonal, 110 error is personal.

Anyone who accepts this idea – and it was once generally accepted – and who wishes to make a contribution to scientific knowledge, will tend to feel it incumbent on him to suppress anything personal or subjective and to present what nature has taught him in an impersonal manner, flatly and authoritatively. I do not say that the biologist whose lecture I mentioned censored his published report because he accepted this idea. On the contrary, I think that he, like most other scientists today, recognizes that all scientific theories are hypotheses 120 which can never be proved (though they may be disproved) by reason and experiment: and that whether or not they turn out to be false, they all originated in the minds of inventive men. But although this old and erroneous philosophical idea has faded out, the style of scientific exposition which it helped to sponsor persists.

Let us turn to the needless difficulties of understanding which didactic dead-pan creates. To grasp a scientific idea it is not enough merely to have a bare statement of it. One has to see its point, see what intellectual demands it satisfies, what problems 130 it bears on, what difference it makes, know something of its prehistory (for instance, earlier attempts in the same area and why they were found unsatisfactory) and something of its contemporary context.

Usually, the person with the best knowledge of an idea's intellectual background is its author. And if he gives a worthwhile account of this background, his account will almost inevitably have an autobiographical flavour. He will explain how he came to perceive a certain problem (for problems are like pieces of furniture: they do not exist by nature, yet they exist 140 objectively, can be examined and described). He will describe his original approach and, perhaps, his earlier attempts to solve it which proved abortive but which helped him to understand it better.

Consequently, if a scientist supposes that it is somehow *de rigueur* to present his ideas in a non-autobiographical and impersonal way, he will hardly be likely to provide the background needed for an adequate grasp of them. If he does not do so, his readers must either be in a position to supply an interpretative context themselves or be unable to understand 150 his ideas at all adequately; and the readers who are in a position to supply this will mostly be his co-specialists. To most people outside his specialism his book will remain a closed book, however laboriously they study it.

It might be objected that what I call didactic dead-pan is really expert's shorthand, the technical slang peculiar to, and readily understood within, a scientific specialism. This objection relies on the optimistic assumption that, when one specialist reads the laconic sentences of a co-specialist, he will supply the *correct* interpretative context for them. This may not be 160 difficult to do in the case of unsurprising results in some well-trodden area of science, but it becomes increasingly difficult the more strange, novel, and far-reaching the new idea is. In the case of an important new idea, didactically presented, it is only too likely that a distorted interpretation of it will get into circulation. If its author does not protest, this may achieve semi-official status and be preserved in text-books and histories of science. Any historian of science who is not just what Collingwood called a scissors-and-paste man can tell of cases of scientific discovery where the story of what really happened lay 170 hidden in diaries and letters, submerged beneath the official legend. Scientific discoveries are remarkable things and we are entitled to the truth about them. It would be better if scientists, instead of relying on some future historian to do it for them more or less inadequately a hundred years later, were to publish the full inside story in the first place.

It is not only natural scientists who are prone to didactic dead-pan: economists, lawyers, marxists and others are at least equally prone. But if natural scientists altogether ceased sounding as if they had been commissioned by the Manufacturer of
180 Nature to compose a few paragraphs of His Handbook, and took to writing in a candid, uncensored, autobiographical way so that most of us could find out what they were getting at, didactic dead-pan would fall into discredit and some of the worst fractures within our culture would gradually mend.

B

29 'Philosophical ancestry' (*line 18*). *Which of these is the most direct ancestor?*

(*a*) Euclid (*b*) Descartes (*c*) Hertz (*d*) Newton (*e*) Popper

8 *According to the writer's* 'paraphrase' (*line 39*), 'analysis' *differs from* 'synthesis'

(*a*) purely in style
(*b*) in making the writer sound less certain
(*c*) in making the reader less self-confident
(*d*) in sounding less conclusive
(*e*) in the methods by which the material is presented

57 'Inductive reasoning', *as the next paragraph points out,*

(*a*) is obviously the same as analysis
(*b*) *can* be expressed in a dogmatic form
(*c*) is, in fact, ultimately a development of Euclid's methods
(*d*) is less conclusive than deductive reasoning
(*e*) is the method of arguing adopted by Descartes

37 *Newton's* 'modesty' (*line 90*) *lies in his* (*choose two*)

(*a*) allegiance to objective standards
(*b*) unemphatic style
(*c*) admission of unoriginality
(*d*) limited claims for his book
(*e*) omission of some important problems

27 *His* 'assurance' (*line 90*) *lies in his* (*choose two*)

(*a*) confident tone
(*b*) disregard of hypotheses

   (c)   refusal to mystify the reader
   (d)   pride in his personal discoveries
   (e)   trust in extra-human standards

48 *Why did Newton write like this? Two possible reasons are given*
   (a)   to refute Descartes
   (b)   to satisfy his deities
   (c)   to express himself subjectively
   (d)   to quell opposition
   (e)   to discount personal fallibility

5 *Since Newton's time the attitude towards scientific discovery has changed; it is now generally accepted that (choose two)*
   (a)   scientists now write quite differently
   (b)   scientific discoveries are, as it were, interim reports
   (c)   scientific discovery depends on the initiative of individuals
   (d)   any scientist can put forward a theory without hesitation
   (e)   reason and experiment are discredited

54 *Even so, the style for most scientific exposition today is*
   (a) archaic (b) persistent (c) outmoded (d) antiquated (e) obsolescent

21 *The main immediate disadvantage which the writer finds in* 'didactic dead-pan' *is that*
   (a)   it isolates scientific ideas from their contexts
   (b)   it omits the human interest
   (c)   it tempts the writer to excessive dogmatism
   (d)   it depreciates the scientist's skill
   (e)   it is difficult to read

45 *Two ultimate disadvantages of* 'didactic dead-pan' *are that (choose two)*
   (a)   most people never understand the ideas at all
   (b)   it creates a habit of using incomprehensible jargon
   (c)   fellow-scientists will misrepresent the ideas to posterity
   (d)   it creates the need for popularizing scientists
   (e)   it can only transmit the dullest ideas

65 *The remark about the* 'Manufacturer of Nature' *(lines 179–180) refers not only to the writer's comment on the style of manufacturers' handbooks, but also to*
   (a)   Descartes's philosophical beliefs

   (*b*)   Euclid's methods of reasoning

   (*c*)   the way a scientist originates an idea

   (*d*)   eighteenth-century theories about the sources of knowledge

   (*e*)   scientific history

10 *The writer's hope is to see*

   (*a*)   a return to a reliance on absolute standards

   (*b*)   less pomposity in any writing

   (*c*)   all forms of censorship removed

   (*d*)   better understanding between scholars of different disciplines

   (*e*)   greater sense of responsibility among popularizing scientists

34 *J. W. N. Watkins's title for his broadcast talk was*

   (*a*)   Humility

   (*b*)   Precision

   (*c*)   Modernization ⎬ is Good for Ideas

   (*d*)   Confession

   (*e*)   Analysis

C *Explain one or more of the following, first 'analytically' and then 'synthetically'*

   1. the mechanism of a bicycle pump

   2. sonata form

   3. money

   4. the reasons for words changing their meaning

   5. democracy

   6. cubism (in painting)

D *Collect examples of 'didactic dead-pan' from contemporary writing. As the writer points out, the disease is not confined to 'natural scientists'.*

E *J. W. N. Watkins unites the two most obvious features of a certain style in the memorable phrase, 'didactic dead-pan'. Christen the styles of some of the writers represented in this book as accurately and memorably as you can in two words each.*

F *Both Professor Stebbing and J. W. N. Watkins write about the expert trying to expound elusive ideas to laymen. Imagine yourself to be the expert now. Exchange an account of some piece of research* *work on your own specialist subject with a schoolfellow who special-izes in another subject. Include as much technical detail as you think your reader can manage – you must not simplify your topic but you must be aware of the difficulties that a layman will experience. Use the full resources of language – as long as they are geared to the topic. At the end, say why you think it is important that your reader should make the effort to follow what you have written.*

14 Style

I

† A review by Ronald Bryden in *The Spectator*, 6 July
   1962

Uneasy Lies the Head by King Hussein of Jordan. Heinemann, 30s

Midway through Muriel Spark's *Ballad of Peckham Rye*, her
daemonic Scots arts graduate, Dougal Douglas, compiles a list
of phrases suitable for inclusion in the autobiography which,
between other employments, he is ghost-writing for an elderly
actress. 'I was too young at the time to understand why my
mother was crying'; 'Memory had not played me false'; 'She
was to play a vital role in my life'; 'Once more fate intervened';
'In that moment of silent communion we renewed our shat-
tered faith'; and – my personal favourite – 'I became the proud
10 owner of a bicycle'.
    Were it not for his moving account of the pains of acquiring
the English and accents of Harrow-on-the-Hill, one would
suspect the author of this memoir of having mastered in the
same northern academy as Miss Spark's horned hero the art of
ghostly cliché. 'I felt', he says, recalling the gift of a splendid
Raleigh from King Feisal of Iraq, 'I would never own anything
more beautiful in my life', and his work is rich in other phrases
hallowed by royal reminiscence. 'Tragedy, the cruellest of all
teachers, helped to transform me from a boy of sixteen into a
20 man'; 'I fought to keep back the tears'; 'Most of us live very
simply'; 'I had perhaps become the son he had always wanted';
'Suddenly I felt very, very lonely'.
    In fact, the style of this work perhaps tells more than King
Hussein – an energetic, brave young ruler, not given to specious
or recriminatory brooding upon historical perspectives – about
the last stage of British imperialism, that of empire by indirect
rule, to which his story and Jordan's belong. There was a

certain splendour in Victorian colonialism: it believed in its
mission of civilising, bringing European education, industry and
30 justice to Asia and Africa. But the period of our mandates in the
Arab world between the wars is a shoddy story of power without responsibility. The client monarchies could do as they liked
in the way of yachts, Rolls-Royces and domestic misrule so long
as they toed the line when British strategic interests were in
question. The monument of the period is Farouk's palace at
Alexandria, with its museums of comic-books and curiosa; this
memoir adds to its documentation with photographs of the
royal Go-Karting stadium at Amman, and a description of how
King Hussein was hauled out of bed in the small night hours to
40 be dressed down by the British ambassador for discharging the
British general of his own army. It seems typical of what the
West has given the Arab world during its years of tutelage that
when the King of Jordan seeks to employ – how shall I say
it? – an English style for his life-story, the best to hand should
be an obvious product of Fleet Street Sunday confession at its
cheapest.

A *Show, by writing down the appropriate letter, which makes the best
sense in each of the nine statements below*

6 *Six sentences are quoted in paragraph I of the review because they are*
(a) epigrams (b) clichés (c) ghosts (d) telling phrases
(e) reminiscences

41 *These six quoted sentences were really written by*
(a) Muriel Spark (b) Dougal Douglas (c) an elderly actress
(d) Ronald Bryden (e) King Hussein

18 *'The author of this memoir' (line 13) is, in Ronald Bryden's
opinion,*
(a) King Hussein (b) Miss Spark's horned hero (c) a master
at Harrow (d) Raleigh (e) a ghost-writer

32 *The first sentence of paragraph 2 tells us that*
(a) a man who writes movingly is unlikely to use clichés
(b) if English is painfully learnt, the writer is unlikely to.
show mastery
(c) good English cannot be learnt in a northern academy

(*d*) the education described in the memoir is not what the style suggests

(*e*) Harrovians are unlikely to write with art

61 *The sense of* 'hallowed' (*line 18*) *is best represented by*

(*a*) made beautiful (*b*) canonized (*c*) made familiar (*d*) remembered (*e*) chosen

3 *The epithet which Bryden would* least *readily apply to King Hussein is*

(*a*) frivolous (*b*) powerful (*c*) fluent (*d*) loyal (*e*) thoughtful

24 *Bryden's sharpest criticism in paragraph 3 is of*

(*a*) the last stage of British imperialism

(*b*) British strategic interests

(*c*) Farouk's palace

(*d*) the British ambassador at Amman

(*e*) Fleet Street

51 *Hussein was fond of*

(*a*) power (*b*) responsibility (*c*) Rolls-Royces (*d*) Go-Karts

(*e*) Sunday confession at its cheapest

12 *The words* 'how shall I say it?' (*line 43*) *indicate that*

(*a*) the following words may offend readers

(*b*) the reviewer considered putting something blunter but rejected the idea

(*c*) the reviewer feels that Hussein really employed a Scottish style

(*d*) the word 'employ' is milder than what the reviewer requires

(*e*) the reviewer is not sure what he means

B *Some of the adjectives below would be suitable as criticisms of some of the twelve sentences quoted in the first two paragraphs. Choose the* four *aptest of these adjectives, and write beside each the sentence which it best suits*

sentimental, untrue, vague, unoriginal, boastful, ungrammatical, unkind, pretentious, ambiguous, overbold, sententious, melodramatic, pompous, unintelligent

C *Write a précis of the third paragraph of the review in 50–75 words.*

D *Write an essay on* Hackneyed Writing *or on* Power without Responsibility.

II

† *Hardy the Novelist*, by Lord David Cecil, 1943

A writer's style, his use of language, is the aspect of his art most illuminating to the critic. For in it we see the relation between inspiration and expression at their closest, most localised and, as it were, most tangible form. Personality appears in a writer's language as it does in the strokes of the painter's brush or the marks of the sculptor's chisel. This is eminently so in Hardy's work. His style is the microcosm of his talent, exhibiting all his faults and virtues in their most characteristic form. Let us examine a passage. Here is a paragraph from the scene in 'A
10 Pair of Blue Eyes' when Knight is clinging to the face of the Cliff without a Name in imminent danger of death, and uncertain whether Elfride will be able to bring help in time to save him:

> He again looked straight downwards, the wind and the water-dashes lifting his moustache, scudding up his cheeks, under his eyelids, and into his eyes. This is what he saw down there: the surface of the sea - visually just past his toes, and under his feet; actually one-eighth of a mile, or more than two hundred yards, below them. We colour according to our moods the objects we survey. The sea
> 20 would have been a deep neutral blue, had happiei auspices attended the gazer: it was now no otherwise than distinctly black to his vision. That narrow white border was foam, he knew well; but its boisterous tosses were so distant as to appear a pulsation only, and its plashing was barely audible. A white border to a black sea – his funeral pall and its edging.
>
> The world was to some extent turned upside down for him. Rain descended from below. Beneath his feet was aerial space and the unknown; above him was the firm, familiar ground, and upon it all that he loved best.
> 30 Pitiless nature had then two voices, and two only. The nearer was the voice of the wind in his ears rising and falling as it mauled and thrust him hard or softly. The second and distant one was the moan of that unplummeted ocean below and afar – rubbing its restless flank against the Cliff without a Name.

E *The next three paragraphs begin*

1. 'No one could call this a piece of faultless writing.'
2. 'Yet his style is capable of greater effects than those of far more competent writers.'
3. 'Further, Hardy had an acute sense of the quality of individual word and phrase.'

   Write three paragraphs, with these opening sentences, **before you read on.**

No one could call this a piece of faultless writing. Hardy says somewhere that, in order to improve his style, he made a study of Addison, Burke, Gibbon, Lamb, Defoe – and *The Times* newspaper. Alas, the only influence I can detect in this passage is that of *The Times* newspaper. It has the heaviness, the stilted-
40   ness, the propensity to refined cliché, of serious journalism. Nor is it even an accomplished example of this ignoble mode of expression. Hardy's lack of craftsman's skill makes him an amateurish journalist. He is always getting tied up in his phrases. Do you notice how he says 'visually just past his toes and under his feet' instead of 'apparently just beneath his toes'? When he wants to state that the sea would have looked blue in happier circumstances, but now looked black, he can think of no better phrase than 'the sea would have been a deep natural blue, had happier auspices attended the gazer: it was
50   now no otherwise than distinctly black to his vision'. Of course, this uncouthness is partly deliberate. His Gothic taste shows itself in his choice of words as much as in his choice of subject. He has a perverse pleasure in crabbedness for its own sake – loves to employ words that most people would avoid; 'domicile' for house, for example, or 'congelation' for freezing, or 'habiliments' for clothes. He even makes an adjective of the last and talks somewhere of a man's 'habilimental' taste, meaning his taste in dress. All this is on purpose; and to criticise it simply as incompetence shows a failure to realise the
60   bent of Hardy's fancy. Still, he was incompetent, too, incompetent in the ordinary mechanics of his trade. He often cannot manage the ordinary syntax and grammar of the English language. He finds it hard to make a plain statement plainly

and he does not improve matters by decking out his misbegotten sentences with faded clichés and genteel circumlocutions.

Yet his style is capable of greater effects than those of far more competent writers. Good style is not a negative thing, dependent for its success on the absence of faults. It succeeds in so far as it gets the author's meaning fully across, in so far as it
70 completely incarnates his conception in the medium of words. Hardy's style can do this, though not always. For one thing, it *is* a style. His strange individuality does contrive to imprint itself on his actual use of language. Even though he uses clichés, the final effect of his writing is never commonplace. His very clumsiness and roughness differentiate it from the leading article, and reveal a characteristic idiosyncrasy in the use of language. You could never mistake a paragraph by Hardy for a paragraph by anybody else. The distinguishing elements in his personality – his integrity, his naïveté, his dignity, his
80 strangeness – are present in the turn of his phrase. And to smooth his sentences out into a polished level of perfection would involve obliterating the mark of Hardy's signature.

Further, Hardy had an acute sense of the quality of individual word and phrase. It shows in the passage I quoted to you from 'A Pair of Blue Eyes': 'The wind and the water-dashes scudding up his cheeks', 'boisterous tosses of the foam'; 'the moan of that unplummeted ocean rubbing its restless flank against the Cliff'. In such phrases the poet in Hardy enables him to rise to a level of expressiveness which many merely
90 competent craftsmen do not get within sight of. His words are the only words for his purpose. I cannot think of any alternative for 'boisterous tosses' or 'rubbing its restless flank' which would give anything like the same effect. Hardy, unexpectedly enough, at such moments has satisfied Flaubert's ideal of style. He has discovered the 'mot juste', the single word which can alone express the shade of meaning he has in mind. His words do more than clothe his conception – they are its embodiment. Nor is it always an easy conception to embody in words: Hardy's conceptions are so intensely imaginative. His words do go
100 beyond his logical meaning to suggest all the subtleties and overtones of the mood in which he regarded it. To the poet's eye he added the poet's finer sensibility to the use of language. The same power shows itself in the movement of Hardy's

114

prose – in its rhythm. It also is often harsh and crabbed, but it
also is intensely expressive. Do you remark how the jerky,
wavering sentences in 'A Pair of Blue Eyes' echo the agitation
in Knight's breast, his quivering suspense, the fragmentary,
spasmodic movement of his thought at this moment of peril?;
the movement of the wind too – 'the wind in his ears, rising and
110 falling, as it mauled and thrust him, hard or softly'? Always
instinctively he modulates sound to make it correspond to the
movement of the emotion it conveys.

F *Compare Cecil's criticism with your own. What valid points does he
make which you omitted? What valid points have you made that he
does not touch on?*

G *Cecil illustrates his final point (lines 110–112) by quoting the
following from* Tess of the D'Urbervilles

'Justice was done, and the President of the Immortals (in
Aeschylean phrase) had ended his sport with Tess. And the
d'Urberville knights and dames slept on in their tombs, unknow-
ing. The two speechless gazers bent themselves down to the
earth as if in prayer, and remained for a long time absolutely
motionless: the flag continued to wave silently. As soon as they
had strength, they arose, joined hands again, and went on.'

Comment on this passage **before you read on.**

Remark how the roll of the first sentence proclaims grandly,
and, as it were, impersonally, the moral of the story. The frustrated rhythm of the next sentence, beginning with the same
grandeur and then cut short, conveys an uprush of emotion,
suddenly checked as by a violent effort of will. Then the straight
narrative goes on, in toneless, abrupt cadence, as if it were the
utterance of a spirit drained by sheer intensity of feeling. This
120 is language used creatively. The truth is, that two elements go
to make a good style. The first is what I may call the element of
understanding: that grasp of the nature of the English language
which enables an author to write it clearly, accurately and
economically. The second is the element of sensibility: that

feeling for the flavour of a word and the flow of a rhythm which
enables him to write it eloquently and expressively. The first
element is intellectual, the child of the critical sense; the second
is aesthetic and is the product of the imagination. Hardy – as
one might expect – has the second in the highest degree, but is
130 noticeably lacking in the first: with the consequence that a
grotesque deficiency in craftsmanship appears in his style side
by side with wonderful strokes of phrase. He writes clumsily;
but he writes creatively.

H *Write an essay on* Style.

III

† *Rehabilitations and other Essays,* by C. S. Lewis, 1939

One day in March, 1781, Mrs. Thrale and Boswell presented
the Doctor with a problem. Had Shakespeare or Milton drawn
the more admirable picture of a man? The passages produced
on either side were Hamlet's description of his father, and
Milton's description of Adam. They run as follows.

> See what a grace was seated on this brow,
> Hyperion's curls, the front of Jove himself,
> An eye like Mars, to threaten and command,
> A station like the herald Mercury
10 New lighted on a heaven kissing hill;
> A combination and a form, indeed,
> Where every God did seem to set his seal
> To give the world assurance of a man.

> His fair large front and eye sublime declar'd
> Absolute rule: and hyacinthine locks
> Round from his parted forelock manly hung
> Clustering, but not beneath his shoulders broad.

It may have seemed a little remarkable that the 'wild genius'
should so abound in classical allusions while the scholar poet
20 was so free from them. But this would surprise no one who was

familiar with the works of both; nor is it the most important difference. It is, in the logical sense, an accident that the figures which fill Shakespeare's description should come from classical mythology. It is their presence and their function, not their source, that matters. The two passages illustrate two radically different methods of poetical description.

I   **Without reading on,** *continue this paragraph by explaining how these two passages illustrate two radically different methods of poetical description.*

Milton keeps his eye on the object, and builds up his picture in what seems a natural order. It is distinguished from a prose catalogue largely by the verse, and by the exquisite choice not
30 of the rarest words but of the words which will seem the most nobly obvious when once they have been chosen. 'Fair large front' – any one, you would say, could think of that. And yet how well it does its work. Those three monosyllables, heavy yet easily uttered, with the glorious vowel of *large*, have already smuggled into our minds the sense of massive, leisurely dignity: it is Michelangelo's Adam 'in that majestic indolence so dear to native man'; we are prepared for the words 'absolute rule' in the next line. Shakespeare's method is wholly different. Where Milton marches steadily forward, Shakespeare behaves
40 rather like a swallow. He darts at the subject and glances away; and then he is back again before your eyes can follow him. It is as if he kept on having tries at it, and being dissatis-fied. He darts image after image at you and still seems to think that he has not done enough. He brings up a whole light artillery of mythology, and gets tired of each piece almost before he has fired it. He wants to see the object from a dozen different angles; if the undignified word is pardonable, he *nibbles*, like a man trying a tough biscuit now from this side and now from that. You can find the same sort of contrast almost anywhere
50 between these two poets. When Milton wishes to convey to us the greatness of Beelzebub he says:

> and in his rising seemed
> A pillar of state. Deep on his front engraven
> Deliberation sat and public care,

And princely counsel in his face yet shone
Majestic, though in ruin. Sage he stood
With Atlantean shoulders, fit to bear
The weight of mightiest monarchies. His look
Drew audience and attention still as night
60   Or summer's noontide air.

But when Cleopatra wants to tell of Antony's greatness, she talks like this:

His legs bestrid the ocean: his rear'd arm
Crested the world: his voice was propertied
As all the tuned spheres, and that to friends;
But when he meant to quail and shake the orb
He was as rattling thunder. For his bounty
There was no winter in't: an autumn 'twas
That grew the more by reaping. His delights
70   Were dolphin like: they show'd his back above
The element they lived in, *etc.*

J Before you read on discuss these two passages on the lines which C. S. Lewis suggests.

You see again how simple, how all of one piece, like the clean growth of a tulip, the Milton is: how diversified – more like a chrysanthemum – is the Shakespeare. In Milton you have first the visual impression; then the moral showing through it; the allusion to Atlas, so obvious that any one (we feel) could have guessed it was coming: finally the stillness, compared, so obviously, so un-cleverly, to night or noon, and yet doing to perfection the work it was meant to do. In Shakespeare, as
80 before, you have the ends of the earth all brought together. You begin with the gigantic hyperbole of a man bestriding the ocean, or an arm cresting the world; you go on to the music of the spheres, to thunder, to the seasons, to dolphins. Nor does one image grow out of another. The arm cresting the world is not a development of the legs bestriding the ocean; it is *idem in alio*, a second attempt at the very same idea, an alternative. The dolphin idea is not a continuation of the autumn idea. It is a fresh start. He begins over again in every second line. If you extract the bare logical skeleton, the prose 'meaning' of each

90 image, you will find that it is precisely the same in most of
them. That is not so with Milton; the prose abstract would
take nearly as many words as the poetical expression. 'Beelzebub was very big; he looked wise; he looked wise though
broken; his shoulders were broad; the people were hushed
when they saw him.' If you do the same to Cleopatra's speech
you get something like this: 'He was great. He was great. He was
great enough to help his friends. He was great enough to hurt
his enemies. He was generous. He was generous. He was great.'
In short, Milton gives you a theme developing: Shakespeare
100 plays variations on a theme that remains the same. In the one,
touch after touch is added to the picture until the whole stands
completed; in the other you get rather a series of lightning
sketches, each of the same subject, and each tossed aside before
the sketcher has really finished. We might distinguish these as
the method of *construction* and the method of *variation*. The first
does one thing as well as it can and then proceeds to the next;
the second cannot do even one thing except by doing it several
times, as if even one thing were inexhaustible, and the poet
could only go on having shots at it until mere necessity forced
110 him to give it up.

It would be a mistake to suppose that what we have here
stumbled on is simply the difference between epic and dramatic
poetry. If I could presume on endless patience I could show
you the opposite. I could take Shakespeare where he is himself
handling epic matter and show that the very same difference
holds between him and Homer as between him and Milton.
I would put the Prologue to the third act of *Henry V*, where
Phoebus is fanning the silken streamers and a city is dancing on
the billows beside Homer's picture of the Greeks advancing 'in
120 silence with their eyes upon their captains'. I would put a dozen
speeches from ancient tragedy beside a dozen speeches from
Shakespeare. Everywhere almost, though not everywhere to the
same degree, we should find the same distinction.

K *Which style of description do you find the more effective?*

L *(Research.) Can you find passages of Shakespeare and Milton which
describe a scene, and see whether they have similar differences?*

M *What are the advantages and disadvantages of analysing short passages as Cecil and Lewis do? Is there a danger of missing the wood for the trees? Can 'style' be isolated in this manner?*

N *Write an essay on* The Critic's Task.

15 Evolution

I

† *The Boundaries of Science*, by Magnus Pyke, 1961

'At Oxford', so the Oxford people put it, 'they ask you what you think; at Cambridge they ask you what you know; and at Edinburgh they ask you what the professor has taught you.' This quotation, I feel, has a direct bearing on the point which we are discussing – namely, the mechanisms by which science is evolving. The progress of science primarily depends on the intellectual capacity of scientists' brains – that is to say, on the efficiency of the organ that they carry in their heads. This is quite clearly a matter of biological evolution. A man's brain is
10 inherited from his parents, and its size and power as a thinking machine depend on his genes just as much as does his stature and the colour of his eyes. And just as the size and complexity of a human brain transcend those of the brain of any other animal, it is possible to conceive that a favourable mutation might take place – perhaps in a century, perhaps in a million years – which would increase the size of the brain of *Homo sapiens* yet further.

On the other hand, this strictly genetical change may never happen. But even if it does not things need not stand still. 'At
20 Cambridge they ask you what you know.' Shakespeare did not know how to fly. We did not have to wait, however, until the slow glacier of mutation and evolution had produced men with wings. Our minds are no more advanced than Shakespeare's, and our arms are certainly not stronger and no more feathery. Yet because we *know* more than Shakespeare did, we are now able to make a machine in which we can fly. Because we possess brains capable of dealing with the abstract ideas of speech and writing, by which we can store away these ideas for later use,

and of mathematics and physics and all the natural sciences –
30 because we can do all this, it almost seems as if by using our
heads we can accelerate evolution at will.

What we know may enable us to achieve things like flying
and travelling under water and, by using radar, moving about
in the dark like bats without bumping into things, but it also
allows us to modify ourselves to suit our environment. We do
not have to evolve a type of man with thick fur to live in Nor-
way, or one specially resistant to heat to drill oil-wells in the
Sahara. By virtue of what we know we can have central heat-
ing in the north and air-conditioning on the equator.

40 But at Edinburgh University, if my quotation may be pur-
sued to its bitter end, they ask you what the professor has taught
you. In any community of creatures, whether they are fruit
flies, guinea pigs, or men, although there is quite a high degree
of genetical uniformity, there is also at the same time a spectrum
of attainment and ability. As I mentioned before, genes,
besides controlling definite factors such as the colour of the
eyes, susceptibility to haemophilia (bleeding disease), or a long
upper lip like that of the Hapsburg kings and queens, also
affect small differences such as gradations in tallness or short-
50 ness. Thus we find, in a community, at one extreme individuals
of the highest intellectual ability – these are the first-class
honours men and women – while at the other end of the scale
there are very dull people. This state of affairs was on one
famous occasion drawn to the public attention in a letter to
The Times containing the following remarkable statement: 'It
may horrify your readers to learn that as many as half the
school-children in the London area possess intelligence quotients
which are below the average.' The point which I want to make,
however, is that an individual possessing what we might call
60 'average' intelligence can be taught just so much.

Shakespeare knew nothing of nuclear physics, but if he were
alive today, he could easily learn as much as the next man.
Isaac Newton was also ignorant about quantum mechanics,
but were he here today would instantly grasp Niels Bohr's
arguments as soon as he made them, and would almost certainly help him to further advances not yet made.

Modern man is able to build on the ideas which his ancestors
have developed and written down. The speed of advance is fast,

because all that has gone before is there for him to learn.
70 Obviously, as each generation passes there are new pieces of
knowledge to learn. And this is the point: we possess minds
which are capable of handling a great deal, but there is a limit
to what the present mind of man can grasp. You cannot teach
a cow to play the violin, neither can you teach a dunce to
understand Einstein's theory of relativity. We may also conclude that there are ideas which cannot be taught even to an
Einstein. For these we may need to await the next step forward
in the biological evolution of the human brain – if this ever
occurs!

80 Sir Julian Huxley has pointed out that 300 million years ago
the only animals with backbones were fish. There were no land
vertebrates. Then, in 70 million years, reptiles were evolved –
dinosaurs, crocodiles, plesiosaurs, ichthyosaurs, pterodactyls,
and tortoises. After more than 100 million years of these, birds
and mammals appeared. The world had 60 million years of
Cenozoic birds and animals, brought to an end by the Ice Age.
Finally, there came man. The question asked by Huxley is
whether it is reasonable for us to hope for any further *biological*
improvement in man as an animal species? The ants were
90 as highly developed 35 million years ago as they are now. Birds
have shown no improvement as flying machines in the last 20
or 30 million years. Perhaps, he suggests, we too have become
biologically stabilized.

Can we then argue that even if man as an animal with a
brain, big though it may be, but only of a certain size, has
become stabilized the fact that he can transmit ideas and experience may be taken as a new mechanism of inheritance? Any
other mammal that is to fly must inherit from its parents a
tendency for long fingers with webbing between them – like a
100 bat no less. We, on the contrary, must inherit the books and
plans in which the way to make an aeroplane is described. And
because experience transmitted in this way is cumulative, the
rate of change becomes faster and faster. Our own age, at the
end of this long line of ideas-collection, is almost the first in
which whole nations have set themselves deliberately to extend
and use scientific and technological knowledge.

The period of evolution into which man has brought himself
by his own efforts can best be described as 'social evolution',

rather than 'biological evolution'. The term 'social evolution'
110 is not entirely apt, because the changes in the achievements of
the species depend predominantly on the intellectual abilities
of mankind arising out of the structure of the human brain and
the use which men make of the products of their brains. It will
serve because the evolutionary effects are only brought to bear
by making use of social organizations. Our ability to fly comes
from the development of aeronautical sciences. Nevertheless,
aeroplanes can only be made by nations organized as industrial
communities. The profound changes in Western society due
to the increasing application of automation similarly depend on
120 the social organization. In the new world of automation when
we shall be economically rich – almost as if we had *all* won
prizes in the football pools – and shall need to spend only a
small proportion of our time in factories and offices, the whole
business will depend on the availability of large amounts of
capital. This collected wealth is a social phenomenon.

But although the social evolution which moves so quickly that
we can actually see it happening is due to brains rather than
biology, it is evolution nevertheless. And the basis of evolution
is the survival of the fittest. This raises a knotty point. Let me
130 quote what the late Professor Joad had to say about it:

> Why does evolution go on, and go on to complicate our structure
> so unnecessarily that, instead of becoming more fitted to our physical
> environment than we used to be, we are less? A degree of adaptation
> which, from the purely physical point of view, would put the average
> human being to shame has been achieved by living organisms
> thousands of years ago. The inference is irresistible, that the achieve-
> ment by life of mere adaptation is not enough, but that living
> beings are evolved at more complicated and therefore more danger-
> ous levels, in the endeavour to attain *higher* forms of life. The amoeba,
140 in short, is superseded by man, not because man is better-adapted
> life, but because he is a better-quality life.

As soon as we talk about 'better quality' in the context of the
scientific facts of evolution we introduce a new factor with
which science does not generally deal. This is the implication of
value, that one kind of creature is better than another – in
short, that one kind of life, with all its attributes of behaviour
and intellectual ability, is at a higher plane, in whatever standards of good and bad we may set, than another. The sciences,

neither physics, chemistry, nor, indeed, biology either, have
150 anything to say about moral values. The tenet of 'the survival of
the fittest' has brought living creatures through the principles
of evolution from the simplest type of animate life, through the
various stages of zoological progression up to the earliest, low-
browed man fashioning stone implements in a cave. The life of
such men has been described as 'nasty, brutish, and short'. We
have come a long way since then. In a short thousand years
well-to-do Europeans have progressed from the draughty castle
to the civilized gentleman's drawing-room. Today, the cumulative advance in scientific knowledge has brought us to the
160 edge of the greatest forward achievement of all.

Evolution in the sciences has so far been part of the new
kind of 'social evolution' derived from men's intellectual capacity. There has been no sign, however, that men's brains have
developed during this period. Einstein knew more than Newton
because he could read what Newton had written, yet his intellectual ability was of the same order. It would be hard to argue,
for that matter, that Newton had a better brain than Aristotle.

Earlier in this chapter I referred to the possibility – it can be
put no higher – that scientific knowledge might one day enable
170 us to arrange a favourable mutation so as to produce, by consciously taking thought to do so, a man with a brain larger and
better than that now possessed by the human species. In fact,
there is no real likelihood that this will become possible – at
least in the foreseeable future.

The genetical pattern by which each one of us is provided
with the mixed characteristics of our ancestors is supplied to the
fertilized cell from which we are developed as a molecule of
deoxyribonucleic acid (DNA). The problem to be solved is to
find the part of this molecule that guides the formation of the
180 brain and discover how it could be beneficially modified. But
here is what Professor Chargaff has to say about the chemistry
of DNA.

A . . . deoxyribonucleic acid consisting of 10,000 nucleotides
(molecular weight 3×10^6) could exist in more than 10^{8000} isomers.
With the, admittedly oversimplifying, assumption that it consists
of trinucleotide tracts of one kind, i.e., adenine-adenine-adenine,
etc., the figure for permutational isomers drops from 10^{8000} to
10^{2000}. But you will agree even so that the nucleic acids may, in

190 their sequences, contain enough code-scripts to supply a universe with information.

But do we have enough intelligence to read the information thus offered to us? Not yet, at any rate. There are people who suffer from giddiness when watching the Milky Way for a long time on a clear night. Such people should not look at the cell nucleus. Where else is there so much in so little? And beyond the range of our perception, this milli-microcosm does not end, but there begin galaxies of invisibility. Still, I say to those who come after us: *Scietis*, you shall know!

200 In plain English this means that we know what the chemical substance that controls heredity is like. It is, in fact, like an immense mosaic picture capable of being assembled in ten-thousand-million-multiplied-by-ten-thousand-million-two-hundred-times-over different ways. Out of all this fantastic number of possibilities we have yet to select the correct design, and having done so, we have then to find out how to change the chemical picture so as to achieve the result we want.

A *In the following summary of the first six paragraphs, fill the gaps with the appropriate words.*

Dr Pyke adapts the opening — **72** [truth/proverb/joke/witticism] to show that science depends for its advance on human intellect and on the — **32** and — **8** [choose two from: intensity/accumulation/desire/hope/development/love/depth/success] of knowledge. The first factor, brains, is — **86** [beyond/within/under/responding to] man's control; it is impossible to predict — **28** [when/whether/how/why] a biological change is going to affect the human brain. On the other hand, because man can — **44** and — **61** [choose two from: discover/record/exploit/discuss/collate/imagine] his findings in language and various scientific systems, he can — **21** [resign/adapt/liken/project] himself to his surroundings in ways that could not be termed — **79** [true/biological/human/intellectual] evolution. However, nature itself imposes a limit on this human activity. The geneticists have shown that, by the working of genes, human beings — **41** [restrict/transmit/impose/limit] not only positive similarities of appearance but also characteristics that — **57** [diverge/vary/change/spread] within a set range; one of these characteristics is intelligence. — 25 [rapid/extensive/limited/dangerous] as is the — 70 [actual/potential/scientific/theoretical] knowledge of the average man in an age of scientific expansion, yet there are limits past which the human mind, at its present biological stage, cannot pass.

B *Reduce the remainder of the passage (lines 80–206) to a summary on the same scale as that given above (that is, to between 200 and 250 words).*

C

Any general argument needs particular examples so as to anchor itself in actual life and include instances to which the reader can assent. He will wish the argument to be derived from some human experience (perhaps the arguer will be inferring some generalization) and he will wish it to be ultimately relevant to human experience (the arguer may be deducing something particular, or even teaching us to act or approach life in a certain way).

On the other hand, unless you are careful, you may find that, in your essays, your argument is all example; you may be basing an argument merely on one or two flimsy observations of your own. If you have met only two redheads in your life, and each was hot-tempered, you will be tempted to generalize that all redheads are hot-tempered. For a small boy, one or two observations (for example the sight of a small girl crying) may quickly turn into a 'truth' ('all girls are cry-babies'). The test you must impose on yourself in your essays is to inspect with care the basis of your argument and the particulars which have helped you to your (possibly limited) opinion.

Let us take an example. Suppose you begin an essay with the resounding statements – 'Shakespeare wrote a large number of plays; of these the best is "King Lear".' *The first statement needs no proof. It is generally accepted that Shakespeare wrote about thirty-seven plays, and no proof is required unless you are addressing your essay to the Baconian society. On the other hand, your second statement – a sweeping opinion of your own – will need to be justified not only by a discussion of the various excellencies of* King Lear *but also by reference to perhaps thirty-six other plays (unless you are going to rely on other authorities).*

We think that Dr Pyke happily marries the particular to the general; occasionally his examples are there to prove a point; more often, he uses particular instances for other purposes. We have listed a number of possible uses of examples, after which we have picked out some of the

examples *themselves. Assign each* example *to one or more* use. *Dr Pyke
uses at least one example for a quite different purpose – say what it is
(or they are). It you can do so without being pompous, explain any joke
under the heading of* (c).

(a) to act as evidence or proof
(b) to suggest a particular instance
(c) as a joke, or light relief
(d) as an analogy, to bring in a helpful comparison from the
     familiar world
(e) to adduce another's authority
(f) to suggest an opposing or contrasting view
(g) to incorporate a telling phrase of another writer (i.e.
     quotation)

49 the opening remark about Oxford, Cambridge and Edinburgh

3 radar (*line 33*)

60 genes (*line 45*)

64 the Hapsburg dynasty (*line 48*)

46 the letter to *The Times* (*line 55*)

54 Sir Julian Huxley (*line 80*)

39 Professor Joad (*line 130*)

76 Hobbes (*if you can find him*)

11 Professor Chargaff (*line 181*)

36 A mosaic (*line 201*)

*To return to the two statements that might have been made about
Shakespeare. If you were trying to convince a Baconian that Shakespeare
wrote Shakespeare, your arguments would be based on textual criticism
and contemporary history, perhaps on cryptography; but if you were
urging the superiority of* King Lear, *you would be arguing along the
lines of dramatic criticism. Different branches of knowledge, in fact,
prescribe their own systems of arguing. Compare a proof of Euclid's with
the arguments of, say, Margaret Rose on page 56 and John Mabbott
on page 1. A historian's argument differs in kind from a physicist's.*

*The following passage is chosen for its relevance to the last passage
and also for its difference; in it D. H. Lawrence seems to be evaluating
life in a way implied by Professor Joad and repudiated by the scientist,
Dr Pyke. But the passage is also remarkable for the particularity of the
writing. Although Lawrence emerges with an 'inexorable law of life'*

(with, it seems, five subsections), he is in fact never far from the tangible and the particular – flowers, people and animals, insects, the sun. The argument, if you can call it such, is the imaginative response to the world of nature. Poets often argue in this way (Keats and Hopkins are two obvious examples). The essay from which this extract comes is entitled, significantly, Reflections on the Death of a Porcupine.

II

† 'Reflections on the Death of a Porcupine', by D. H. Lawrence (in *Selected Essays*), 1925

Life moves in circles of power and of vividness, and each circle of life only maintains its orbit upon the subjection of some lower circle. If the lower cycles of life are not *mastered*, there can be no higher cycle.

In nature, one creature devours another, and this is an essential part of all existence and of all being. It is not something to lament over, nor something to try to reform. The Buddhist who refuses to take life is really ridiculous, since if he eats only two grains of rice per day, it is two grains of life. We did not make

10 creation, we are not the authors of the universe. And if we see that the whole of creation is established upon the fact that one life devours another life, one cycle of existence can only come into existence through the subjugating of another cycle of existence, then what is the good of trying to pretend that it is not so? The only thing to do is to realize what is higher, and what is lower, in the cycles of existence.

It is nonsense to declare that there is no higher and lower. We know full well that the dandelion belongs to a higher cycle of existence than the hartstongue fern, that the ant's is a higher

20 form of existence than the dandelion's, that the thrush is higher than the ant, that Timsy, the cat, is higher than the thrush, and that I, a man, am higher than Timsy.

What do we mean by higher? Strictly, we mean more alive. More vividly alive. The ant is more vividly alive than the pine-tree. We know it, there is no trying to refute it. It is all very well saying that they are both alive in two different ways, and therefore they are incomparable, incommensurable. This is also true.

But one truth does not displace another. Even apparently
30 contradictory truths do not displace each other. Logic is far too coarse to make the subtle distinctions life demands.

Truly, it is futile to compare an ant with a great pine-tree, in the absolute. Yet as far as *existence* is concerned, they are not only placed in comparison to one another, they are occasionally pitted against one another. And if it comes to a contest, the little ant will devour the life of the huge tree. If it comes to a contest.

And, in the cycles of *existence*, this is the test. From the lowest form of existence, to the highest, the test question is: *Can thy neighbour finally overcome thee?*
40 If he can, then he belongs to a higher cycle of existence.

This is the truth behind the survival of the fittest. Every cycle of existence is established upon the overcoming of the lower cycles of existence. The real question is, wherein does *fitness* lie? Fitness for what? Fit merely to survive? That which is only fit to survive will survive only to supply food or contribute in some way to the existence of a higher form of life, which is able to do more than survive, which can really *vive*, live.

Life is more vivid in the dandelion than in the green fern, or than in a palm tree.
50 Life is more vivid in a snake than in a butterfly.

Life is more vivid in a wren than in an alligator.

Life is more vivid in a cat than in an ostrich.

Life is more vivid in the Mexican who drives the wagon, than in the two horses in the wagon.

Life is more vivid in me, than in the Mexican who drives the wagon for me.

We are speaking in terms of *existence*: that is, in terms of species, race, or type.

The dandelion can take hold of the land, the palm tree is
60 driven into a corner, with the fern.

The snake can devour the fiercest insect.

The fierce bird can destroy the greatest reptile.

The great cat can destroy the greatest bird.

The man can destroy the horse, or any animal.

One race of man can subjugate and rule another race.

All this in terms of *existence*. As far as existence goes, that life-species is the highest which can devour, or destroy, or subjugate every other life-species against which it is pitted in contest.

This is a law. There is no escaping this law. Anyone, or any
70 race, trying to escape it, will fall a victim: will fall into subjugation.

But let us insist and insist again, we are talking now of existence, of species, of types, of races, of nations, not of single individuals, nor of *beings*. The dandelion in full flower, a little sun bristling with sun-rays on the green earth, is a nonpareil, a nonesuch. Foolish, foolish, foolish to compare it to anything else on earth. It is itself incomparable and unique.

But that is the fourth dimension, of *being*. It is in the fourth dimension, nowhere else.
80 Because, in the time-space dimension, any man may tread on the yellow sun-mirror, and it is gone. Any cow may swallow it. Any bunch of ants may annihilate it.

This brings us to the inexorable law of life.

1. Any creature that attains to its own fullness of being, its own *living* self, becomes unique, a nonpareil. It has its place in the fourth dimension, the heaven of existence, and there it is perfect, it is beyond comparison.

2. At the same time, every creature exists in time and space. And in time and space it exists relatively to all other existence,
90 and can never be absolved. Its existence impinges on other existences, and is itself impinged upon. And in the struggle for existence, if an effort on the part of any one type or species or order of life can finally destroy the other species, then the destroyer is of a more vital cycle of existence than the one destroyed. (When speaking of existence we always speak in types, species, not individuals. Species exist. But even an individual dandelion has *being*.)

3. The force which we call *vitality*, and which is the determining factor in the struggle for existence, is, however, derived
100 also from the fourth dimension. That is to say, the ultimate source of all vitality is in that other dimension, or region, where the dandelion blooms, and which men have called heaven, and which now they call the fourth dimension: which is only a way of saying that it is not to be reckoned in terms of space and time.

4. The primary way, in our existence, to get vitality, is to absorb it from living creatures lower than ourselves. It is thus transformed into a new and higher creation. (There are many ways of absorbing: devouring food is one way, love is often 110 another. The best way is a pure relationship, which includes the *being* on each side, and which allows the transfer to take place in a living flow, enhancing the life in both beings.)

5. No creature is fully itself till it is, like the dandelion, opened in the bloom of pure relationship to the sun, the entire living cosmos.

D *D. H. Lawrence's argument is not logical in form but proceeds by a series of swoops; hence it is difficult sometimes to be sure of the connexions between one part of the argument and another. Here is a summary of this passage down to line 79. Fill in the gaps with connecting words taken from the list given at the bottom; you will have to use some words twice.*

It is an inescapable fact of nature that all creatures feed on other creatures in order to keep alive. — 81 the inconsistency of the Buddhist, — 19 even he has to destroy some life in order to subsist. — 73 it is pointless to shut our eyes to this process of universal rapine. We ought, — 31, to recognize, in the interests of our survival as a species, that there are higher and lower forms of existence. — 69 are these distinctions rendered meaningless by the argument that animal life differs in kind from plant life. This argument is true, of course, — 7 by no means contradicts the principle that all forms of life compete with each other. — 51, different as is an ant's life from a pine-tree's, the ant is ultimately strong enough to destroy the pine-tree. — 65 it is of a higher cycle of existence.

What is the goal of this universal struggle? Is there no other aim than to overcome, or be overcome by, weaker, or stronger, forms of life? — 16 is there some culminating purpose for the highest form of life? These are questions one would naturally ask, — 84 they ignore a crucial distinction. In speaking of higher or lower cycles of existence we refer to a whole species, considered as existing in time and space. — 45, as even the dandelion at the bottom of the scale can show us, there is a different quality – *being* – which is outside time and only occurs when an individual member of a species is perfectly itself.

but, for, hence, however, indeed, nor, or, rather, therefore

E *How might a Buddhist and a logician reply to D. H. Lawrence's remarks about them?*

F *Explain carefully what of D. H. Lawrence's original passage has been lost in the summary.*

G *On what does D. H. Lawrence base his argument?*

H *Imagine that D. H. Lawrence and Dr Pyke and you are members of a Brains Trust. Judging from these two passages, how might the two of them give brief answers to the following questions? And what would you say?*

    1. How far does modern science entitle us to use the word 'progress'?

    2. How do you account for genius?

    3. Is the human species changing?

    4. What departments of human life are beyond the reach of science?

I *Compare the styles of the two writers.*

J *'The sciences, neither physics, chemistry, nor, indeed, biology either, have anything to say about moral values' (Pyke, line 148). Having commented on the grammar of this sentence, write an essay on its meaning.*

K *Write on or discuss* Individuality.

Further reading

CHARLES DARWIN, *The Origin of Species*, 1859.

JULIAN HUXLEY, *Evolution in Action*, Chatto & Windus, 1953; Penguin (Pelican).

G. G. SIMPSON, *The Meaning of Evolution*, Oxford University Press, 1950.

G. S. CARTER, *A Hundred Years of Evolution*, Sidgwick & Jackson, 1957.

H. GRAHAM CANNON, *The Evolution of Living Things*, Manchester University Press, 1958.

JOHN MAYNARD SMITH, *The Theory of Evolution*, Penguin Books (Pelican), 1958.

The ideas of D. H. LAWRENCE are best seen as he presents them imaginatively in his poems, his short stories, and his novels. Of the latter *The Rainbow* (rev. edn., Heinemann, 1926), is not easy but is rewarding.

16 Culture

I

† *Notes towards the Definition of Culture*, by T. S. Eliot, 1948

The primary channel of transmission of culture is the family: no man wholly escapes from the kind, or wholly surpasses the degree, of culture which he acquired from his early environment. It would not do to suggest that this can be the only channel of transmission: in a society of any complexity it is supplemented and continued by other conduits of tradition. Even in relatively primitive societies this is so. In more civilised communities of specialised activities, in which not all the sons would follow the occupation of their father, the apprentice
10 (ideally, at least) did not merely serve his master, and did not merely learn from him as one would learn at a technical school – he became assimilated into a way of life which went with that particular trade or craft; and perhaps the lost secret of the craft is this, that not merely a skill but an entire way of life was transmitted. Culture – distinguishable from knowledge about culture – was transmitted by the older universities: young men have profited there who have been profitless students, and who have acquired no taste for learning, or for Gothic architecture, or for college ritual and form. I suppose that something of the
20 same sort is transmitted also by societies of the masonic type: for initiation is an introduction into a way of life, of however restricted viability, received from the past and to be perpetuated in the future. But by far the most important channel of transmission of culture remains the family: and when family life fails to play its part, we must expect our culture to deteriorate. Now the family is an institution of which nearly everybody speaks well: but it is advisable to remember that this is a term

that may vary in extension. In the present age it means little
more than the living members. Even of living members, it is a
30 rare exception when an advertisement depicts a large family or
three generations: the usual family on the hoardings consists of
two parents and one or two young children. What is held up for
admiration is not devotion to a family, but personal affection
between the members of it: and the smaller the family, the more
easily can this personal affection be sentimentalised. But when
I speak of the family, I have in mind a bond which embraces a
longer period of time than this: a piety towards the dead, however obscure, and a solicitude for the unborn, however remote.
Unless this reverence for past and future is cultivated in the
40 home, it can never be more than a verbal convention in the
community. Such an interest in the past is different from the
vanities and pretensions of genealogy; such a responsibility for the
future is different from that of the builder of social programmes.

A

17 'Culture' *here means*

    (a) knowledge of the arts
    (b) a way of life based on a respect for the past
    (c) knowledge of skills developed in the past
    (d) family environment
    (e) the lessons taught by a university

10 *How many channels or conduits, transmitting culture, does the writer
mention?*

    (a) one (b) two (c) three (d) four (e) more than four

38 *By comparison with* 'channels', *the writer feels that* 'conduits'
(*line* 6) *are* (*choose two*)

    (a) artificial (b) effective (c) continuous (d) secondary
(e) insignificant

78 *The word* 'even' (*line* 7) *implies that one would expect relatively
primitive societies*

    (a) to practise no education outside the family
    (b) to be superstitious
    (c) not to know how to record tradition
    (d) not to be included in any discussion of culture
    (e) to be rich in various traditions

20 *At the end of his fourth sentence (lines 7–15), the writer complains of today's*
(a) blinkered specialization (b) low standards of craftsmanship (c) irreligion (d) filial disobedience (e) loss of discipline

56 *A merit of the* 'older universities' *(line 16) was that*
  (a) all students developed deep academic interests
  (b) students learnt about the arts
  (c) all students unconsciously were aware of traditions
  (d) all students consciously were aware of traditions
  (e) all students, whether consciously or unconsciously, were aware of traditions

6 *The writer says of* 'societies of the masonic type' *(line 20)*
  (a) they will last into the future
  (b) they do not encourage interest in Gothic architecture or college ritual
  (c) they open up careers for young men
  (d) their publicity is skilful
  (e) they pass on a valuable tradition

62 *The writer suggests that our view of* 'the family' *has become*
  (a) healthy (b) antiquated (c) irreverent (d) admirable (e) restricted

24 *Which of these come closest to the writer's concept of a family?*
  (a) pride in one's family tree
  (b) the welfare state
  (c) love of parent for child
  (d) a devotion to positive tradition
  (e) a passion for the cultivation of the past

52 'A verbal convention in the community' *(line 40) means*
  (a) old-fashioned habits of speech
  (b) a claim stated but not felt
  (c) a basis for social reform
  (d) religious belief
  (e) a matter for debate

B *For discussion*
  1. What can we learn of value today from primitive communities?
  2. How do advertisements affect our ways of thinking?
  3. What are the dangers of a small family?
  4. What are the uses of a museum?

II

† 'Does Culture Matter?' (in *Two Cheers for Democracy*), by E. M. Forster, 1951

Cultivated people are a drop of ink in the ocean. They mix easily and even genially with other drops, for those exclusive days are over when cultivated people made only cultivated friends, and became tongue-tied or terror-struck in the presence of anyone whose make-up was different from their own. Culture, thank goodness, is no longer a social asset; it can no longer be employed either as a barrier against the mob or as a ladder into the aristocracy. This is one of the few improvements that have occurred in England since the last war. The change has
10 been excellently shown in Mrs Woolf's biography of Roger Fry; here we can trace the decay of smartness and fashion as factors, and the growth of the idea of enjoyment.

All the same, we are a drop in the ocean. Few people share our enjoyment so far. Strictly between ourselves, and keeping our limited circulation in mind, let us put our heads together and consider for a moment our special problem, our special blessings, our special woes. No one need listen to us who does not want to. We whisper in the corner of a world which is full of other noises, and louder ones.
20 Come closer. Our problem, as I see it, is this: is what we have got worth passing on? What we have got is (roughly speaking) a little knowledge about books, pictures, tunes, runes, and a little skill in their interpretation. Seated beside our gas-fires, and beneath our electric-bulbs, we inherit a tradition which has lasted for about three thousand years. The tradition was partly popular, but mainly dependent upon aristocratic patronage. In the past, culture has been paid for by the ruling classes; they often did not know why they paid, but they paid, much as they went to church; it was the proper thing to do, it was a form of
30 social snobbery, and so the artists sneaked a meal, the author got a sinecure, and the work of creation went on. To-day, people are coming to the top who are, in some ways, more clear-sighted and honest than the ruling classes of the past, and they refuse to pay for what they don't want; judging by the

noises through the floor, our neighbour in the flat above doesn't
want books, pictures, tunes, runes, anyhow doesn't want the
sorts which we recommend. Ought we to bother him? When he
is hurrying to lead his own life, ought we to get in his way like
a maiden-aunt, our arms, as it were, full of parcels, and say to
40 him, 'I was given these specially to hand on to you ... Sophocles,
Velasquez, Henry James . . . I'm afraid they're a little heavy,
but you'll get to love them in time, and if you don't take them
off my hands I don't know who will . . . please . . . please . . .
they're really important, they're culture.'

His reply is unlikely to be favourable, but, snubbing or no
snubbing, what ought we to do? That's our problem, that's
what we are whispering about, while he and his friends argue
and argue over the trade-price of batteries, or the quickest way
to get from Balham to Ealing. He doesn't really want the stuff.
50 That clamour for art and literature which Ruskin and Morris
thought they detected has died down. He won't take the parcel
unless we do some ingenious touting. He is an average modern.
People to-day are either indifferent to the aesthetic products of
the past (that is the position both of the industrial magnate and
of the trade unionist) or else (the Communist position) they are
suspicious of them, and decline to receive them until they have
been disinfected in Moscow. In England, still the abode of
private enterprise, indifference predominates. I know a few
working-class people who enjoy culture, but as a rule I am
60 afraid to bore them with it lest I lose the pleasure of their
acquaintance. So what is to be done?

It is tempting to do nothing. Don't recommend culture.
Assume that the future will have none, or will work out some
form of it which we cannot expect to understand. Auntie had
better keep her parcel for herself, in fact, and stop fidgeting.
This attitude is dignified, and it further commends itself to me
because I can reconcile it with respect for the people arguing
upstairs. Who am I that I should worry them? Out of date
myself, I like out of date things, and am willing to pass out of
70 focus in that company, inheritor of a mode of life which is
wanted no more. Do you agree? Without bitterness, let us sit
upon the ground and tell sad stories of the death of kings, ourselves the last of their hangers-on. Drink the wine – no one wants
it, though it came from the vineyards of Greece, the gardens

of Persia. Break the glass – no one admires it, no one cares any more about quality or form. Without bitterness and without conceit take your leave. Time happens to have tripped you up, and this is a matter neither for shame nor for pride.

80 The difficulty here is that the higher pleasures are not really wines or glasses at all. They rather resemble religion, and it is impossible to enjoy them without trying to hand them on. The appreciator of an aesthetic achievement becomes in his minor way an artist; he cannot rest without communicating what has been communicated to him. This 'passing on' impulse takes various forms, some of them merely educational, others merely critical; but it is essentially a glow derived from the central fire, and to extinguish it is to forbid the spread of the Gospel. It is therefore impossible to sit alone with one's books and prints, or to sit only with friends like oneself, and never to testify outside.

90 Dogmatism is of course a mistake, and even tolerance and tact have too much of the missionary spirit to work satisfactorily. What is needed in the cultural Gospel is to let one's light so shine that men's curiosity is aroused, and they ask why Sophocles, Velasquez, Henry James should cause such disproportionate pleasure. Bring out the enjoyment. If 'the Classics' are advertised as something dolorous and astringent, no one will sample them. But if the cultured person, like the late Roger Fry, is obviously having a good time, those who come across him will be tempted to share it and to find out how.

100 That seems to be as far as we can get with our problem, as we whisper together in our unobtrusive flat, while our neighbours, who possess voices more powerful than our own, argue about Balham and Ealing over our heads. Remember, by the way, that we are not creative artists. The creative artist might take another line. He would certainly have more urgent duties. Our chief job is to enjoy ourselves and not to lose heart, and to spread culture not because we love our fellow men, but because certain things seem to us unique and priceless, and, as it were, push us out into the world on their service. It is a Gospel, and 110 not altogether a benign one; it is the zest to communicate what has been communicated. Works of art do have this peculiar pushful quality; the excitement that attended their creation hangs about them, and makes minor artists out of those who have felt their power.

C *Here is a very free paraphrase of E. M. Forster's essay. Pick out the most appropriate word from each quartet.*

Formerly the wealthy rulers of England — **75** [aspired/condescended/were delighted/were reluctant] to employ artists, not out of — **15** [sympathy/a sense of duty/a desire for fame/kindness] but because convention dictated it. In twentieth-century democracy, however, when the new rulers can see little use for the arts, most people — **48** [attack/ridicule/ignore/belittle] the artistic achievements of the past in favour of more — **30** [spectacular/important/selfish/immediate] useful interests. The few who are devoted to culture cannot offer it — **66** [firmly/solemnly/fussily/apologetically] to the — **2** [philistine/flippant/purposeful/foolish] majority without fear of meeting a — **42** [groan/complaint/laugh/rebuff] or a yawn; nor can they shut themselves off from the world in coteries and, in their nostalgia, — **26** [commit/ally/surrender/resign] themselves to superannuation. For culture cannot be restricted to cliques; it — **59** [impels/reminds/forbids/asks] its enthusiasts to proselytize. The most effective course for them, therefore, will be to — **13** [exaggerate/parade/display/control] their enjoyment so as to — **82** [badger/stimulate/convince/dismay] the unconverted; then these may find out what they are missing. Thus can the enthusiasts, urged on by the — **34** [value/force/religion/enjoyment] inherent in all great works of art, help to pass on their message.

D *This version may retain the plain meaning of the original but it jettisons all the implications and the emotional attitudes. How does the writer feel towards the rulers of the past, the 'average modern', and the enthusiasts? How can you tell? What does the humour of the original convey?*

E *Show the variety of E. M. Forster's style by picking out both the 'literary' features of style (e.g. quotation, aphorism, resounding generalization, antithesis) and the colloquialisms.*

F *Compose a script for a broadcast talk to last five minutes, in which you develop the same point that E. M. Forster makes about culture on behalf of either* Religion *or* Writing verse.
The dangers are timidity, priggishness and bogus heartiness.

G *T. S. Eliot and E. M. Forster obviously mean different things by the word 'culture'. What does each mean? And what are the implications of each of their arguments?*

17 Punishment

I

† *A Fearful Joy*, by Joyce Cary, 1949

Both women look anxiously at the small boy as at a dangerous small animal. Tabitha says in her severest tone, 'Now John, you know what I said would happen if you went on being a nuisance to nurse.'

John, having turned to the basin, is swimming the soap-dish in it. There can be seen in his expression not only the obstinacy but the cunning of a four-year-old who joins the intelligence of a small boy to the complete egotism of a baby.

'Answer me, John.' Tabitha takes him by the arm. 'You hear
10 what I said; do you want to be smacked?'

John adds the sponge-bowl to the soap-dish, and keeps silence. Tabitha turns pink, wrinkles appear between her brows; and in the young face there appears suddenly the shadow, the hint of an old woman, an old woman, it is said, of character; that is, one who has acquired from her battles a strong will and decided opinions, rather than resignation.

'Do you hear, John? Answer me at once.'

The two women exchange a glance; both are aware of the supreme quality of the crisis. For a slap is the last resort. After
20 the slap, there is nothing. A slap is the old guard, and if it fail, the battle is lost; anarchy must come.

Tabitha's glance is really an appeal to the nurse for support, for some brilliant decision which will save the last terrible risk. But at such moments the supreme commander is always alone. The nurse's expression says clearly, 'You've threatened that slap before, and now you must do it; the consequence is not my responsibility.'

'Very well, John.' Tabitha takes the child's arm and draws him away from the basin.

30 'For the last time, John.'

But he says not a word. Tabitha, quite infuriated with this obstinacy which is, she perceives, pure wickedness, an evil will enjoying itself, puts him across her knee and gives him two hard slaps.

There is pause and awful silence. Is John going to win? Tabitha holds her breath. But suddenly a loud cry is heard; a protesting wail. Tabitha's face clears, she smiles with relief; and hastens to take John on her knee.

'Now, darling, it was your own fault.'

40 'I'm sorry, Mum,' the boy howls.

'You see what happens if you're naughty.' But she kisses him, a weakness which causes the nurse to turn away with a look meaning, 'Oh, these mothers.'

'Yes – Mummy.'

'And now if you're really good again – are you good?'

'Oh yes-ss, Mummy, I'm good.'

'You shall have a chocky.'

Two minutes later, John, with the virtuous expression of one reconciled, purged of sin, and renewed by grace, is eating 50 chocolate. But he remembers, now and then, to embrace Tabitha, to assure her that he is good again, and to assure himself that this powerful person is once more well inclined to him. The powerful person, full of gratitude to those mysterious forces which have secured her victory, returns the kisses with warmth. For the gratitude, seeking expression, naturally finds part of its object in John.

Afterwards nurse congratulates the commander-in-chief.

'That was just what he needed, Mum; it was in the nick.'

'Yes, I thought the time had come; it would be easy to 60 spoil Johnny.'

A *Choose the best alternative*

4 'anxiously' (*line 1*) *because*

    (*a*) they are frightened on his behalf

    (*b*) they fear he may turn against them

   (c) they doubt whether their wills can prevail over his

   (d) they are not sure what he is thinking

   (e) each woman is uncertain whether the other will support her

50 *John is swimming the soap-dish (line 5) to express*

   (a) disobedience (b) nonchalance (c) anxiety (d) curiosity (e) excitement

22 *Which of the following sentences about John is* not *implied?*

   (a) he insists on having his own way

   (b) he counts on the women's unwillingness to smack him

   (c) he refuses to cooperate

   (d) he does not know what will happen

   (e) he is quick at sizing up the position

67 *Tabitha reminds the writer of an old woman of character (line 14) because*

   (a) she wants to frighten John

   (b) experience has taught her to be firm

   (c) she is re-living her mother's experiences

   (d) her friends think her mature

   (e) she considers giving in to John

12 *The crisis is acute because (choose two)*

   (a) a slap is a severe punishment

   (b) after a slap nothing will happen

   (c) a slap represents action after many threats

   (d) slapping is old-fashioned

   (e) if John is unmoved by the slap, they will not be able to control him

   (f) a slap is a form of self-defence

   (g) to slap John is to turn the affair into a fight

35 *The most important emotion revealed by Tabitha's behaviour after the slapping is*

   (a) fondness for John

   (b) regret at having hurt him

   (c) anxiety to be friendly with him again

   (d) relief at his reactions

   (e) keenness that the nurse should not misunderstand her

B *Is Tabitha's behaviour reasonable?*
What part does emotion play in her actions? What is the effect of the
nurse's presence?
What is Tabitha's motive in punishing John?

C *What is the author's own attitude? Contemptuous? Sympathetic?*
Ironical? Do his comments tell you anything about his views on
punishment? How sincere is his use of military and theological
expressions?

D *Do you agree with the description of John's behaviour as pure*
wickedness?

E *Write the account of the affair given afterwards*
1. by John 2. by the nurse

II

† *Fear, Punishment, Anxiety and the Wolfenden Report,* by
Charles Berg, 1959

The old theories advanced to explain the phenomenon of legal
punishment are obviously rationalizations and do not merit
detailed consideration. We have space to select only a few typical
examples, and to subject them merely to a very brief review.

The Prison Commissioners, under the long Chairmanship of
Sir E. Ruggles-Brise – it lasted from 1895 to 1920 – evidently felt
that their duty was to justify the existing order. They tried to
combine all theories and principles in the supreme object –
punishment. 'Prisons exist for punishment,' they said. The chief
principles involved in punishment were said to be:

        (i) Retribution
        (ii) Deterrence
        (iii) Reform.

To take these in order:

Retribution.

The then Archbishop of York, in the rôle of penal reformer,
made the following public statement: 'The first duty of the

State is to dissociate itself from the act of its own member; to do this it must act, not only upon but against that member. . . .
20 His act implicates the community, unless the community repudiates it. The community must exhibit an antagonism in its will against the will of the offending member. This is necessary for the preservation of its own character on which the character of its citizens largely depends.'

It would appear from this that it is necessary for us to emphasize by retributive punishment that we, for our part, repudiate the criminal act. If this aggressive repudiation is necessary, it amounts to a confession that otherwise we should be liable to do the act ourselves. What other need can there be
30 for punitive repudiation, for this violent denial of condonement, unless it be that our position is insecure – that our own temptation to do likewise is a menace to our ego-control?

If this is indeed true, would it not be more appropriate to punish our own criminal id, to punish ourselves, instead of seeking this way out at the expense of a scapegoat?

Do we not thereby actually express upon him our own hate impulses – to teach him that hate impulses must on no account be expressed; and to ensure that we ourselves will not express them!

The attempt to justify retribution as reasonable is mani-
40 festly absurd. That the retributive element exists in the psychology of punishment there is no denying. It is an emotional force. I would criticize merely the attempt to rationalize it, to justify it, and to disguise it as a function of the reason.

In tracing the evolution of modern punishment, Prof. Hamon, of Brussels, starts with what he calls the reflex instinct of defence. To this succeeds vengeance, or the reaction at a longer interval. This, he says, is the basis of the most primitive of laws, the lex talionis. Finally the law of retaliation (retribution) is developed and codified.

F *Neutrally stated, the first two paragraphs amount to this:*
Some theories about legal punishment seem to me to be attempts to justify by reason an attitude that is, in origin, emotional. I will mention and review one or two of them.

The Prison Commissioners in the early part of this century did not propose changes, but treated punishment as valid in itself; they held that its principles were (i) Retribution (ii) Deterrence (iii) Reform.

1. *List the words in the first two paragraphs of the extract which colour this neutral statement, and discuss the effect of each. You might begin*

'Old' and 'advanced' are legitimate words, but could also carry overtones ('old' = old-fashioned, 'advanced' = put forward in a specious way).

'Phenomenon' implies at the start that legal punishment is strange, a process that could not have been logically arrived at . . . etc.

> *Do these additions improve the argument, in your view, by making it more persuasive and forceful? Or do they diminish its effect by revealing the writer's own emotions so clearly?*
>
> *Discuss in general terms the place of rhetoric and indignation in presenting a case, by comparison with a cold and dispassionate approach. What are the advantages and disadvantages of each?*

G *Discuss the following views*

1. 'Repudiation is necessary for the preservation of the community's own character, on which the character of its citizens largely depends.'

2. 'Repudiation by means of punishment is a confession that otherwise we should be liable to do the act ourselves.'

> *Does the second follow from the first (as the writer implies)? Or does it deny the first? Or ignore the first?*

H *Express in your own words Berg's central point in this section (lines 25–35).*

I Defence – vengeance – lex talionis – retaliation – retribution. (Hamon)

Preservation of the community's integrity – repudiation – retribution. (William Temple, Archbishop of York)

These two sequences are quite different in kind. How? Construct two sequences both ending in the word 'conscience' but otherwise differing as sharply as Hamon's and Temple's. To what extent can two men who use these two different approaches have an argument? What difficulties would a psychologist find in writing about Freedom of Choice, *or a theologian in writing about* The Importance of Evolution?

J *Write Berg's next paragraph (on* Deterrence) *for him.*

III

† *The Doctrine of Atonement,* by Leonard Hodgson, 1951

There are sometimes said to be four different theories of punishment: retributive, vindictive, deterrent and reformatory. But of these the last two are not, strictly speaking, theories of punishment at all. Laws limiting the hours at which alcoholic drinks may be sold may be both reformatory and deterrent, they may aim at deterring drunkenness and improving the dietary habits of a people; we should not call them punitive unless they were enacted in view of existing culpable inebriety When we are punishing, we may seek to punish in such a way as to reform
10 and to deter. In so doing we are seeking to combine those other aims with that of punishing. It is the retrospective element that makes the action punishment. Moreover, the door may be opened to injustice, and to unjustifiable interference with a man's right to run his own life, if we cease to pay heed to such sayings as 'Let him alone; he's been punished enough.'

The idealists, then, are right in contending that punishment is essentially retributive and vindictive. But the meaning to be given to these words requires careful examination. Without some further explication of its nature, I am not happy about
20 the phrase 'punishment is an end in itself' – a phrase commonly used by idealists in reaction against its definition as a means to deterrence or reformation. And left to themselves the words 'retributive' and 'vindictive' are only too apt to suggest paying a man back in his own coin or wreaking vengeance. Indeed, this latter understanding of them is directly encouraged by writings representing all schools of thought and dating from the period of the authors from whom I have quoted. It was then the fashion to seek to explain all human psychological and sociological phenomena in terms of evolutionary genetics, and
30 punishment was assumed to be the corporate expression of a primitive instinct of revenge. The idealists sought to maintain that in being taken over by the community the expression of this instinct was somehow purged of its viciousness and transformed into a manifestation of righteousness. Their opponents denied

this and denounced it as exhibiting the indelible character of its vicious origin.

But about the same time Pringle-Pattison, in his Gifford Lectures for 1912 and 1913, was undermining the ground common to both parties in the dispute. He showed that in evolution
40 we have to recognise *both* the continuity of the process *and* the coming into existence of real differences of kind. I want now to maintain that, whatever may be the truth about its psychological history, there is an absolute difference of kind between punishment and anything in the way of 'hitting back' or vengeance. Those who connect the two fall into confusion through failing to take note of the fundamental truth about punishment, *that it is an activity which by its very nature can only exist between a community and a member of itself.* In a spirit of revenge one man can hit back at another man, or one state at another state, but
50 so long as they are acting simply as fellow citizens, or fellow sovereign states, man cannot punish man, or state state. It is not enough to say that they ought not to; in the nature of things they cannot. When one man claims to be inflicting punishment on another, it can only really be punishment if, like a judge, he has the authority to act in the name of the community to which both belong.

Each man is born into his individual existence as a member of a family. Through his family he is a member of the local community, of the nation-state, of the human race. As he grows
60 he receives membership in other communities: he may be reborn into the Christian Church, he may be enrolled in a school, a college, the ordained ministry of the Church, the civil service or the armed forces of his country, a business firm or a labour union. It is impossible for any human being to act in a purely individual capacity. The only life he has, that which makes him what he is, is what comes to him through his membership in these various communities; it is that share in the common life with which he is entrusted, for which he is responsible. He cannot divest himself of his representative character without ceas-
70 ing to be the man he is. I who write this am an Englishman, a priest of the Church of England, a professor of the University of Oxford. God grant that I may not so behave or speak as to lead my fellow countrymen to say: 'That is the sort of man that makes one ashamed of being British.'

The individual represents the community. The community is represented by the individual. But there is a limit. The freedom of the individual member to direct his share of the common life in accordance with his own decisions is balanced by the freedom of the community to disown and dissociate itself from those
80 of his utterances and acts which contradict what it stands for. Punishment is essentially this disowning by a community of acts done by its members.

Consider the case of a father whose young son has been detected in an act of dishonesty. He may cudgel his wits in an attempt to discover some way of making clear to him without any unpleasantness that this is not the sort of thing the family stands for. But he may as well save himself the trouble, for it cannot be done. The expression of the fact, if it is to be effective, must inevitably be painful. Hence the inseparable connection
90 between the ideas of punishment and pain. Where there is possibility of variation is in the degree and manner of the pain to be inflicted. Here four factors have to be considered: (i) the necessity for clear and unambiguous disapproval; (ii) the degree of abhorrence merited by the evil deed; (iii) the possible need of aiming at deterring other potential evil-doers; and (iv) the duty of aiming at the reformation of the miscreant. Of these the last two need no further comment. The second is the safeguard against unjustifiable interference with a man's right to run his own life. The first requires some further attention.
100 It is in the interests of the wrongdoer himself that the community should disown and dissociate itself from connivance at his evil acts. If the thieving or lying boy is smiled upon in the family circle for his cleverness, what prospect has he of restoration to share in honest living when he comes to a better frame of mind and repents of what he has done? He has dragged the family down with him to his lower level; it is no longer where it was for him to get back to. Its manifest repudiation of what he has done is the means whereby it maintains its goodness in spite of the fact that some of its own life and energy have been
110 engaged in doing evil.

Repeating what I have written elsewhere, I may add that it may help to show that the principles I have attempted to set forth are not mere *a priori* speculation, if we reflect that they are, as a matter of fact, the principles on which our social life

is actually lived. Two illustrations must suffice. If a member of
a football team is deliberately guilty of 'dirty play', it is the
team which is held responsible. The good name of the team
depends on its disowning the act of the individual player.
Again, the safety of any one of us when travelling or residing
120 abroad rests on the fact that the government of the land in
which we are will be held responsible by our own government
for any attacks made upon us by its citizens. The principle of
collective responsibility, guarded against the misuse of individual liberty by collective acts of disapproval and repudiation,
is the cornerstone not only of the cleanliness of sport and the
peace of the world, but of the whole moral stability of mankind.
　　Punishment is in essence the means whereby a community
maintains the standards by which it seeks to live without in-
hibiting the vocation of its members to develop their own per-
130 sonal freedom. Rightly understood and administered, it avoids
on the one hand indifference to moral values and on the other a
regimenting of human life which ignores the human rights of
individual persons. It is the counter-balancing of the freedom of
the individual to run his own life by the freedom of the community to repudiate his transgressions of its standards. Thus it is
both retributive and vindictive, but not in the sense of paying
back or taking revenge. As applied to punishment, the word
'retributive' simply means that it is action which looks back to
something already done; it is the guarantee of each man's right
140 to run his own life as he thinks fit until he has done something
which gives the community ground for invading his freedom.
The word 'vindictive' must be understood as a contraction of
vindicative; it means that the action is taken for the purpose of
vindicating the standard that has been jeopardised by the
evil deed.

K *Which words make the best sense in this general summary of the first
two paragraphs?*

The — 83 [essence/entity/zenith/quality] of punishment is that
it looks back to an — 33 [object/outrage/inebriety/offence]; it is
not — 55 [legal/legitimate/legislative/liberal] to punish with the
— 40 [past/present/future/criminal] alone in view, since that

which — **68** [condones/forbids/allows/justifies] punishment is — **9** [desert/reformation/deterrence/drunkenness] and nothing else. Deterrence and reformation cannot therefore be — **74** [implicit/ integral/innate/inbred] elements of punishment, though once we have the — **58** [duty/right/desire/urge] to punish we may well seek — **27** [instead/at least/also/indeed] to reform and to deter. So — **43** [ideally/in principle/in origin/in theory] punishment is retributive and vindicative; yet, because of the — **63** [implications/associations/suggestions/coinage] of these two words, — **14** [doubts/reactions/meanings/misunderstandings] arise if they are not carefully — **53** [defined/limited/phrased/controlled]. For they suggest — **80** [genetics/punishment/sociology/revenge] as the — **23** [motive/purport/phenomenon/fashion] of punishment; and until recently most — **47** [idealists/psychologists/utilitarians/ thinkers] agreed that punishment had this — **77** [basis/expression/fashion/purpose], even though it had become a — **5** [primitive/corporate/vicious/righteous] matter. Whether they affirmed or denied that this — **71** [changed/exhibited/affected/maintained] its present — **29** [status/efficiency/manifestation/application], they agreed in — **37** [allowing/accounting/apologizing/ answering] for it as having — **85** [diminished/been transformed/ developed/appeared] from something — **18** [primitive/revolutionary/phenomenal/unworthy].

L 'Punishment is an activity which can only exist between a community and a member of itself' (*line 47*).

Do you agree? If so, discuss

1. a trade embargo
2. a father's reduction of his son's allowance
3. a man's refusal to speak to a neighbour who has wronged him
4. a restaurant exercising its right not to serve a drunken customer
5. a libel case with punitive damages

If not, refute Hodgson's argument.

M *List the communities which you represent, and find a situation in which you specially represent each of them. Are there any situations in which you are not representing any of them?*

N 'The last two need no further comment' (*line 97*). *Why not? Have you any further comment on them?*

O *Define* 'collective responsibility', 'punishment', 'retribution', *and* 'vindictive', *as Hodgson would define them. Which word does he employ in an unusual sense?*

P *Which of Hodgson's illustrations seems to you the most effective, and why?*

Q 'It avoids on the one hand indifference to moral values and on the other a regimenting of human life which ignores the human rights of individual persons' (*line 130*). *Discuss.*

R *Which of these views of punishment seems to you the more cogent? Do any practical consequences follow from the ordinary man's attitude to punishment?*

S *Is it possible to agree with Hodgson and yet press for the abolition of Capital Punishment? Explain the line of argument that you would use.*

T *Is it possible to agree with Berg, and yet believe it right that those who break laws should be punished? Explain the line of argument that you would use.*

U *Distinguish between the following pairs of words*

      retribution – retaliation
      reformative – remedial
      deter – dissuade
      rationalization – explication
      existing – traditional
      disown – repudiate
      condone – forgive
      victim – scapegoat
      abhorrence – disapproval

V *Write an essay on* A Writer's Choice of Words.

W *Berg and Hodgson both imply that the views which they themselves do not hold are old-fashioned. In what circumstances is a view in fact discredited by being old-fashioned? Is there too much emphasis on intellectual fashions in discussion, so that we too readily ask whether a* *view is* 'contemporary' *or* 'outmoded' *rather than whether it is true or false? (For further discussion of this see the first of C. S. Lewis's* Screwtape Letters.) *Write an essay on* Intellectual Fashions.

X *Write a talk which you as headmaster would give to your prefects, explaining why and how they are to punish,* OR *why and how the school will in future be run without punishment being used.*

18 Modern Arts

You might prepare yourself for this chapter by doing one or more of the following

1. Look at your school buildings, and at buildings in the neighbourhood, particularly modern ones. What do you think of them? Why do you think that about them? How much prejudice colours your choice?

2. Go to an art gallery, or any place where pictures, particularly those recently painted, are hung. Again, what are your reactions? How prejudiced are they?

3. Re-read any poem that you enjoy and see how much of it is realistic, and how much, on the other hand, is fanciful and decorative.

4. Think how you would define the phrase 'modern music'. How much would your definition include – jazz, pop music? Have you listened to any music, recently composed, that you think is not ephemeral?

It may be helpful to sort out in advance one's prejudices about modern arts, for these prejudices are apt to be dogmatic, not to say hysterical. Moreover, as viewers of pictures, listeners to music, promenaders through a new town, readers of books, we are very suspicious of the critics of these arts; we should probably defer to a plumber or a motor mechanic when our drains or our cars go wrong, more readily than to a music critic or an English don when a modern piano concerto or novel sets our teeth on edge. The three passages that follow all attack prejudices that may alienate people from the arts of today. Well, not quite today. The passages were written between 1934 and 1941 (we have given the date of each). It may be that events have since proved the writers wrong or trite; it may be that the prejudices they attack are still entrenched.

I

† *The Scientific Attitude*, by C. H. Waddington, 1941

As far as subject matter goes, painters have on the whole shown more sympathy for science than have poets. There are many pictures whose whole subject matter is more or less scientific. The dream images and unconscious associations used by the surrealists of course existed before they were scientifically studied, but it is only since psychologists became interested in them that the world in general has been willing to give them much attention, and it is doubtful whether surrealism would have been taken up as a 'movement' in recent years if Freud
10   had not lived. 'For we surrealists,' says Salvator Dali, 'as you will easily see if you pay us the slightest attention, are not exactly artists and neither are we exactly true men of science.'

The subject matter of most abstract pictures is even more clearly chosen from the objects well known to science. Some artists, such as Ben Nicholson and Mondrian, use mainly the simplest and most perfectly geometrical shapes, such as circles, straight lines and rectangles. Others use more complex scientific concepts, such as series of lines which define a curve or a surface which is technically known as their envelope; one sees
20   them in the paintings of Erni and some of the recent drawings and carvings of Barbara Hepworth. It is significant that the English abstract artists invited a scientist, Bernal, to contribute to their International Survey of Constructive Art, 'Circle'. He pointed out two further uses made by artists of scientific thought; the use of the more subtle relations of symmetry, and the use of irregular shapes which are not arbitrary but which are defined by some algebraic function, so that they might be a graph of some imperceptible physical quality, such as a distribution of electric charge.
30   These are some of the uses of science as subject matter by artists. It is in more fundamental respects that the influence of science has been really important. In the first place, the whole of what has been called above the destructive activity of the last twenty years was an essential prerequisite to the creation of a

scientific style. Science is essentially analytical. It can look at
any phenomenon, from something as cold and empty of significance as the orientation of a molecule on a surface, to the
bearing of a man whose head is bloody but unbowed. But it
must get its items separated; anything subjected to its scrutiny
40 must be isolated from the mush of general goings-on in which
it is normally embedded; it must be defined, or if it cannot be
formally defined, at least one must be able to indicate what
exactly is the thing one is talking about, and what else is the
fortuitous rag-tag-and-bobtail that happens to be cluttering it
up at the moment. And, after the twenty or thirty centuries of
culture which we consciously inherit, everything was pretty
completely mixed up with everything else. We had, as Picasso
said, infected the pictures in our museums with all our stupi-
dities, all our mistakes. Can anyone still hear God Save the King
50 or the Star-Spangled Banner as a tune? Each is covered so deep
with associations that our ears can hardly disentangle it. If a
young man falls in love, the chances are that he finds his imagination cluttered up with a tedious rigmarole of roses and
moonlight and so on. It was from science that the advice came
to sort out the welter into its component parts; to separate the
sexual physiology from the botany and meteorology.

Moreover the associations and prejudices which had clus-
tered round each item of straightforward experience, and were
smothering them as ivy smothers a tree, were derived from the
60 old world which at the end of the first World War was already
tottering under the impact of science, and must soon be altered
out of all recognition by it. The focal points of our social life
should have noble embodiments, said the pundits; a bank
should be built in the classical style, a railway station perhaps
in Gothic. But, answered common sense, hacking away a few
chunks of ivy, we are not living in the eighteenth century's
imitation of classical Greece, nor do engine drivers necessarily
aspire to reach Heaven by solitary contemplation and mor-
tification of the flesh. Honour thy father and thy mother, said
70 the fifth commandment; but scientific psychology showed that
honour was hardly an adequate way of dealing with the com-
plexities of family life. Love is a sacrament, the romantic poets
cried; but science, leading off in the first round with that
troublesome customer by cutting down most of the tree along

with the ivy, said that love was a psychological corollary of a particular hormone balance, and Aldous Huxley's characters let it go at that.

> Had they deceived us
> Or deceived themselves, the quiet-voiced elders,
80 Bequeathing us merely a receipt for deceit?

asks Eliot in a poem published quite recently. The world was already saying 'Yes' twenty years ago. And loud in the chorus was the voice of science.

If the old meanings clustering round our daily life were dead; if ancestral wisdom was a fraud or no longer applied; if society was sick, and we had purged it to its bare bones, where were we to turn for new values, fresh food to bring the convalescent back to health? We have seen the surrealist solution. Objects peeled of the coatings of emotion with which generations of
90 human experience have covered them become ghosts of themselves, and can live a phantasmal life hovering on the lunatic fringe of consciousness, producing in men the vacuous mental excitement of paranoia. The only other alternative to the grime of the outworn past is to consider things not as concretions of other men's thoughts and feelings about them, but as agents which produce effects in the world. To consider them, in fact, scientifically. If the moon is a body giving off light of such and such a wavelength and such and such an intensity, there is no smear of sentimentality over its face. Light of that colour and
100 that brightness can be significant and moving, not because we have been told that the Moon is the Goddess of Love, but perhaps because it abolishes differences of colour and fineness of detail from what we see; or because we experience it at the same time as silence and a relief from the necessity of doing something soon; or even possibly for some more obscure reason to do with the habits of life of our biological ancestors.

The scientific attitude to the world does not in the slightest deny the emotional effects produced on men by their experience; what it tries to do is to classify the mechanisms by which these
110 effects were produced. Some will be more, some less and some very little, dependent on associations inherited from the culture of the past. If the more culturally dependent are rejected, what is left is an immediate effect, directly related to the circum-

stances of the actual experience, not fictitiously heightened by a
plausible reference to some general but spurious theory. Consider, as an example of a modern love lyric, a verse by Auden:

> Lay your sleeping head, my love,
> Human on my faithless arm;
> Time and fevers burn away
> Individual beauty from
> Thoughtful children, and the grave
> Proves the child ephemeral;
> But in my arms till break of day
> Let the living creature lie,
> Mortal, guilty, but to me
> The entirely beautiful.

120 marks the line position.

In every phrase the poet is emphasising his refusal to consider
the girl as anything but an ordinary girl, insisting on her normal
humanity, and in the last line but one specifically rejecting, for
130 himself, the concepts 'mortal, guilty' with their theological
connotations; but no one would claim that because of this
matter-of-factness the poem is lacking in feeling.

A *Which is the nearest synonymous word or phrase to the word given,
as used in the passage?*

23 'Sympathy' (*line 2*)
(*a*) pity (*b*) enthusiasm (*c*) consideration (*d*) fellow-feeling

107 'Arbitrary' (*line 26*)
(*a*) chosen at random (*b*) thought-out (*c*) rational (*d*) chosen
deliberately

63 'Fortuitous' (*line 44*)
(*a*) chance (*b*) untidy (*c*) lucky (*d*) superficial

14 'Rigmarole' (*line 53*)
(*a*) collection (*b*) mumbo-jumbo (*c*) formula (*d*) mess

44 'Pundits' (*line 63*)
(*a*) the experts (*b*) the so-called experts (*c*) the best authorities (*d*) pompous politicians

73 'Aspire' (*line 68*)
(*a*) try (*b*) intend (*c*) make it their ambition (*d*) strive (*e*)
expect

18 'Concretions' (*line 94*)

(*a*) substances that have grown large (*b*) objects overlaid with foreign matter (*c*) aggregates (*d*) sum total

54 'Sentimentality' (*line 99*)

(*a*) glamour (*b*) sickliness (*c*) false emotion (*d*) romantic associations

3 'Fictitiously' (*line 114*)

(*a*) vividly (*b*) fancifully (*c*) misleadingly (*d*) ingeniously

101 'Spurious' (*line 115*)

(*a*) specious (*b*) of doubtful origin (*c*) fallacious (*d*) absurd (*e*) outmoded

B *The argument gains an impetus from the linked references and elaborate metaphors with which the writer leads the eye and mind forward. To what single word does each of these phrases or words look back?*

48 'Meterology' (*line 56*)

82 'Classical style' (*line 64*)

22 'Aspire to reach heaven . . . flesh' (*line 68*)

106 'That troublesome customer' (*line 74*)

41 'Convalescent' (*line 87*)

C *How important to the argument is the writer's choice of* clutter, ivy, sickness, dirt *for metaphors?*

D *Here are some of the writer's opinions expressed in the passage. Pick the relevant words.*

The Surrealist Movement developed because — **75** [artists/the public/psychologists] came to — **10** [doubt/appreciate/paint] the psychological importance of — **66** [certain key images/ paintings/Freud].

Waddington — **87** [abuses/admires/enjoys/disapproves of] Surrealist art because it — **28** [stimulates a futile horror in the viewer/helpfully strips objects of irrelevant associations/directs our minds to the spiritual world/results merely from a scientific theory].

(*N.B. The writer discusses Surrealist art in two places.*)

Waddington is — **95** [inconvenienced by/amused at/impatient with] people who define love in — **70** [magical terms/vague abstractions/psychological jargon] and surround it with — **93** [glamorous/botanical/sentimental/pleasant] images.

Science has not only cleared human traditions of their — **38** [pomposity/grandeur/inessentials/simplicity] but also — **59** [ignored/disproved/ridiculed/questioned] many of those traditions themselves.

Waddington — **79** [begs/orders/advises] artists today to — **6** [penetrate/see through/disperse] the haze of sentiment that surrounds natural objects and — **90** [evaluate/analyse/ignore] their effects on human experience.

Artists should not — **35** [falsify/induce/disturb/intensify] the emotional effect of their works with — **98** [ancient/distasteful/antiquated] conventions.

E *Write down in about 100 words what Professor Waddington thinks are the functions of art today.*

II

† *Introduction to Modern Architecture,* by J. M. Richards, 1940

There have been so many misunderstandings about modern architecture that before we begin to discuss what it is, it may be as well to mention a few things that it is not. It is not, for one thing, a fashionable style of jazz ornament; it is not the custom of building in concrete, or with flat roofs and horizontal window-panes: it is not 'functionalism'. It *is* quite simply, like all good architecture, the honest product of science and art. It aims at once more relating methods of building as closely as possible to real needs. In fact it is nothing more nor less than
10 the exact modern equivalent of the architecture that flourished in previous ages, but fell into decay during the last century through architects having got out of touch with life and having forgotten what architecture was really for.

There are several other reasons why it is important just now for the Man in the Street to understand a little more what this modern architecture is all about, besides the reason of satisfying his own curiosity and justifying the architects who produce it. One reason is that, like all movements that contain something new as well as something important, the modern move-
20 ment in architecture has acquired a following of imitators: vulgarizers who join up with the movement only in order to cash in, as it were, on its news value. To this category belong all the makers of jazz-modern shop-fronts in chromium plate and glass, all the purveyors of smart angular furniture and all the builders of nasty 'modernistic' villas; people who have no understanding of the new architecture but would not have come into being without it. This bogus modernism, whether it is the result of the commercial exploitation of novelty or merely the wish to be in the fashion, obviously does great harm to the
30 cause of good modern architecture. It brings it into disrepute. And the only way to prevent the fine ideals of the one from being vulgarized into insignificance by the other is for people to discriminate better between them. If people understand the point of genuine modern architecture and appreciate what it is trying to do, they will see quickly enough that the un-genuine – which is often called 'modernistic' – has no basis beyond itself. It consists only of a few flashy tricks and the use (often the wrong use) of a number of fashionable materials.

It will be objected that if the real modern architecture repre-
40 sents the revival of architecture as an art, and the bogus modern architecture is only a few flashy tricks, it should be easy enough to tell them apart, because the former will be beautiful and moving – in fact will have the qualities of a work of art – while the latter will appear what it is: trivial and vulgar. One answer is, unfortunately, that we cannot rely on our own good taste. The state of architecture and the design of nearly everything around us has sunk so low that we are no longer capable of judging what is good. We have become so bewildered by the various and meaningless structures that have been put up for a
50 hundred years in the name of architecture, that we have ceased to look at buildings with the eyes with which one should look at a work of art. Instead we have become accustomed to look at the superficial trappings of architecture and admire them or

otherwise as ornamentation – and even then not with our eyes but with our minds. We judge them according to a literary standpoint, and only think about whether they look imposing or romantic or antique, or whether they conform correctly to certain 'styles'. Or else we do not look at all, but shrug our shoulders and say that we suppose these architects know
60 what they are about; it is all very mysterious and professional. So one answer is that we simply have not the ability to discriminate about architecture, because we have no real aesthetic standards to judge by. In fact we have no taste, only habits – and generally bad habits. We shall only acquire taste by taking pains to develop our visual sensibility and our knowledge.

Another answer is that in all but a few cases even the best modern architecture has at present only a limited amount of positive appeal to our eyes. It will take time to get used to it; and, moreover, at the stage the modern architects' experiments
70 have now reached they still find themselves spending a large proportion of their energy eradicating the old bad habits from the practice of architecture. Having succeeded in getting away from the imitation of the styles of previous centuries, they are often content to be severely practical and aesthetically inoffensive. Perhaps, apart from wanting to proceed only one step at a time, they have been anxious to begin by emphasizing the aspects of their own architecture that mark it most clearly as different from the kind that went before. For whatever reason, modern architecture has been passing through a sort of 'puri-
80 tan' phase, in which the negative virtues of simplicity and efficiency have been allowed to dominate. The important thing in the future is that modern architecture should blossom into full maturity without losing the sincerity which is at present its special virtue, or the inevitability which it gets from its appearance being so closely related to its structure. It must not become merely decorative: an imitation of itself.

Already the imitation and the real often get mixed up. Buildings with good qualities use bad materials, or make experiments that do not come off; and some public understanding of the basis
90 on which modern buildings are designed would at least make it easier for a good standard to be established. It is not suggested, however, that good intention should be admitted as an excuse for bad performance, or that knowing how it got like that will

make a bad building better. Architecture, besides being a social art, is a visual art, and aesthetic judgment must be independent of intellectual knowledge. But neither will it help to disparage the ideals of modern architecture on account of failings due to immaturity. That would only discourage perseverance.

F

45 *Richards discusses*

    (*a*) Victorian (and post-Victorian) architecture

    (*b*) cheap modern architecture

    (*c*) serious modern architecture

    (*d*) an ordinary man's feelings towards modern architecture

    Which of the following adjectives would he most readily apply to (a)? to (b)? to (c)? to (d)? (Use each adjective once.)

austere, basic, functional, jaded, meretricious, modish, plain, prejudiced, pretentious, stylized, submissive, tawdry

G *Juxtapose phrases of Richards with those of Waddington which mean exactly the same thing. Hence, briefly show how far Richards on architecture agrees with Waddington on painting and poetry.*

H *Distinguish between Richards's attitude to his reader* (hectoring? pleading? rhetorical? didactic? confident? cautious?) *and his attitude to those who vulgarize modern architecture* (contemptuous? impatient? tolerant? sorrowful? like a picnicker plagued with wasps?).

I *What exactly does Richards want his reader to do about modern architecture?*

J *Précis the passage in not more than 360 words.*

III

† *Music, Ho!* by Constant Lambert, 1937

Revolutionaries themselves are the last people to realize when, through force of time and circumstances, they have gradually become conservatives. It is scarcely to be wondered at if the

public is very nearly as slow in the uptake. To the public a red
flag remains a red rag even when so battered by wind and
weather that it could almost be used as a pink coat. Nothing is
so common as to see a political upheaval pass practically un-
noticed merely because the names of the leaders and their
parties remain the same. Similarly in the world of music, the
10 fact that some of the key-names in modern music, such as
Stravinsky and Schonberg, are the same as before the war has
blinded us to the real nature of the present-day musical revolution. We go on using the words 'revolutionary composer' just as
we go on using the words 'Liberal' and 'Bolshevik'; but between the modern music of pre-war days and that of today lies
as much difference as that between the jolly old Gilbertian
'Liberal or Conservative' situation and the present mingled
state of the parties, or that between the clear anarchical issues
of the October Revolution and the present situation in Russian
20 politics with Stalin at the head of a frustrated Five Year Plan
and Trotsky in exile.

To the seeker after the new, or the sensational, to those who
expect a sinister *frisson* from modern music, it is my melancholy
duty to point out that all the bomb throwing and guillotining
has already taken place. If by the word 'advanced' we mean
art that departs as far as possible from the classical and conventional norm, then we must admit that pre-war music was
considerably more advanced (if that is any recommendation)
than the music of our own days. Schonberg's *Erwartung*, for
30 example, still the most sensational essay in modern music from
the point of view of pure strangeness of sound, was actually
finished in 1909. If your ear can assimilate and tolerate the
music written in 1913 and earlier, then there is nothing in post-
war music that can conceivably give you an aural shock, though
the illogicality of some of the present-day pastiches may give
you a 'rare turn' comparable to the sudden stopping of a lift
in transit.

We are most of us sensationalists at heart, and there is something rather sad about the modern composer's relapse into good
40 behaviour. There is a wistful look about the more elderly
'emancipated' critics when they listen to a concert of contemporary music; they seem to remember the barricades of the
old Russian Ballet and sniff plaintively for blood. The years that

succeed a revolution have an inevitable air of anti-climax, and
it is noticeable that popular interest in the Russian Soviet films
has considerably waned since the directors turned from the joys
of destruction to the more sober delights of construction. With
the best will in the world we cannot get as excited about *The
General Line* as we did about *Potemkin*, and it is doubtful if any
50 of the works written since the war will become a popular date in
musical history, like those old revolutionary warhorses *Le Sacre
du Printemps* and *Pierrot Lunaire*.

But it is only the more elderly emancipated critics who have
lived through both campaigns, so to speak, and who realize the
subtle difference between the two. There is a large mass of the
public that has only become modern-music conscious since the
war, and they are hardly to be blamed if they lump the two
periods together as 'all this modern music'.

During the war people had sterner things to think of than
60 Schonberg, and a concert of his works would have been not
only impracticable, but unpatriotic. The general cessation of
musical activities during the war resulted in many pre-war
works only becoming known a considerable number of years
after they were written. This may seem platitudinous, but it
should be remembered that it would not be necessarily true of
literature. If Joyce, for example, had written and published
Anna Livia Plurabelle in 1913, there would have been nothing,
theoretically speaking, to prevent it from becoming familiar to
every schoolboy by about 1919; but the number of people who
70 can read a modern score is fewer even than the number who
claim that they can, and the more extreme examples of modern
music cannot be grasped without several actual hearings. Moreover, the printing of literature is not the same as the playing
of music. Any printer can print *Ulysses* (if the law lets him), but
not every orchestra can play *Erwartung*. It is regrettable, but
hardly surprising, that this work had to wait sixteen years for
its first performance.

K

27 *Summarize, in your own words, three reasons why most people were
unable, between 1914 and 1934, to acquaint themselves with modern
music.*

L

56 *List the words that remind us of the physical details of a political revolution. Why this harping?*

M *Give examples of epigram and irony. What impression do you receive of Constant Lambert's personality?*

N *Briefly annotate this passage so as to identify for a reader all the historical, musical, literary and cinematic references.*

O *Have the gramophone and tape-recorder helped overcome the objections of Constant Lambert's last paragraph? (Later in* Music Ho! *there is a chapter about the wireless and gramophone called* 'The Appalling Popularity of Music'.)

P *In what are the writers of the three extracts agreed?*

Q *Compare the manner and the style of the three writers.*

R *Has anything occurred since these passages were written that supports or denies their theses?*

S *What are the possibilities of modern sculpture? Bear in mind certain social needs and the new materials that are the by-products of science.*

T *In what ways can the arts interpret human experience and assist human needs?*

U *Bearing in mind the arguments you have just read, on what principles would you*

    1. design a car park to serve a local shopping centre?
    2. write a poem about a robin?
    3. design a coffee-pot?
    4. acquaint yourself with a work of Schonberg's which you have never heard but which a friend of yours calls 'one hell of a racket'.

V *Here are three poems written in the twentieth century. Are they modern in a Waddingtonian sense? What do they set out to do? And what, if any, pleasurable impact do they make?*

    1.   'nine birds . . .'

        nine birds (rising

        through a gold moment) climb:
        ing i

-nto
wintry
twi-

light
(all together a
manying
one

-ness) nine
souls
only alive with a single mys-

tery (liftingly
caught upon falling) silent!

ly living the dying of glory
                              e. e. cummings

2.   RESTORING GENDER

A thousand thousand mewling poets cried of you this:
'Lady, Luna; Phoebe, female; Blue Bulger, Shrinker;
O Woman O, O shadow forth – with thy waxing
Or (rhyme clinking) waning – a Virgin Queen or
                                        some quean
Moony, Mothery, Mistressy, Mysterious.'

'Lack Lyly, 'lack Keats, this Faithful Shepherdess
Is but a Thing, no She, nor no Man in her,
Nor is't, oh, a Male, as our grunt Anglo-
Saxon ancestor huffed
And hummed, or mumbled
And fumbled with clown charms
Weird at Wapentake:
'Hoo, hurr. Moon, Mona, He.'

Neither Man nor Woman but a Thing.
Circumference 8000 miles: put that straight,
Ready too and fit
For our Child's first dart going off
Onto, into, It.
                              Francis Berry

3.   IN TIME OF WAR   VIII

He turned his field into a meeting-place,
And grew the tolerant ironic eye,
And formed the mobile money-changer's face,
And found the notion of equality.

And strangers were as brothers to his clocks,
And with his spires he made a human sky;
Museums stored his learning like a box,
And paper watched his money like a spy.

It grew so fast his life was overgrown,
And he forgot what once it had been made for,
And gathered into crowds and was alone,

And lived expensively and did without,
And could not find the earth which he had paid
    for,
Nor feel the love that he knew all about.
                              W. H. Auden

W *Auden's poem perhaps describes successive stages in man's civilization. At what stage does modern man enter the poem? Does the
writer's diagnosis challenge Waddington's argument at any point?*

19 Society and the Individual

I

† *On Liberty*, by J. S. Mill, 1859

Though society is not founded on a contract, and though no good purpose is answered by inventing a contract in order to deduce social obligations from it, every one who receives the protection of society owes a return for the benefit, and the fact of living in society renders it indispensable that each should be bound to observe a certain line of conduct towards the rest. This conduct consists first, in not injuring the interests of one another; or rather certain interests, which, either by express legal provision or by tacit understanding, ought to be considered
10 as rights; and secondly, in each person's bearing his share (to be fixed on some equitable principle) of the labours and sacrifices incurred for defending the society or its members from injury and molestation. These conditions society is justified in enforcing at all costs to those who endeavour to withhold fulfilment. Nor is this all that society may do. The acts of an individual may be hurtful to others, or wanting in due consideration for their welfare, without going to the length of violating any of their constituted rights. The offender may then be justly punished by opinion, though not by law. As soon as any part of
20 a person's conduct affects prejudicially the interests of others, society has jurisdiction over it, and the question whether the general welfare will or will not be promoted by interfering with it, becomes open to discussion. But there is no room for entertaining any such question when a person's conduct affects the interests of no persons besides himself, or needs not affect them

unless they like (all the persons concerned being of full age, and the ordinary amount of understanding). In all such cases there should be perfect freedom, legal and social, to do the action and stand the consequences.

30   It would be a great misunderstanding of this doctrine to suppose that it is one of selfish indifference, which pretends that human beings have no business with each other's conduct in life, and that they should not concern themselves about the well-doing or well-being of one another, unless their own interest is involved. Instead of any diminution, there is need of a great increase of disinterested exertion to promote the good of others. But disinterested benevolence can find other instruments to persuade people to their good, than whips and scourges, either of the literal or the metaphorical sort. I am the last person to
40 undervalue the self-regarding virtues; they are only second in importance, if even second, to the social. It is equally the business of education to cultivate both. But even education works by conviction and persuasion as well as by compulsion, and it is by the former only that, when the period of education is past, the self-regarding virtues should be inculcated. Human beings owe to each other help to distinguish the better from the worse, and encouragement to choose the former and avoid the latter. They should be for ever stimulating each other to increased exercise of their higher faculties, and increased direction of their
50 feelings and aims towards wise instead of foolish, elevating instead of degrading, objects and contemplations. But neither one person nor any number of persons, is warranted in saying to another human creature of ripe years, that he shall not do with his life for his own benefit what he chooses to do with it. He is the person most interested in his own well-being; the interest which any other person, except in cases of strong personal attachment, can have in it, is trifling, compared with that which he himself has; the interest which society has in him individually (except as to his conduct to others) is fractional,
60 and altogether indirect: while, with respect to his own feelings and circumstances, the most ordinary man or woman has means of knowledge immeasurably surpassing those that can be possessed by any one else. The interference of society to overrule his judgment and purposes in what only regards himself, must be grounded on general presumptions; which may be altogether

wrong, and even if right, are as likely as not to be misapplied
to individual cases, by persons no better acquainted with the
circumstances of such cases than those are who look at them
merely from without. In this department, therefore, of human
70 affairs, Individuality has its proper field of action. In the conduct of human beings towards one another, it is necessary that
general rules should for the most part be observed, in order that
people may know what they have to expect; but in each person's
own concerns, his individual spontaneity is entitled to free
exercise. Considerations to aid his judgment, exhortations to
strengthen his will, may be offered to him, even obtruded on
him, by others; but he himself is the final judge. All errors
which he is likely to commit against advice and warning, are
far outweighed by the evil of allowing others to constrain him to
80 what they deem his good.

I do not mean that the feelings with which a person is regarded
by others, ought not to be in any way affected by his self-
regarding qualities or deficiencies. This is neither possible nor
desirable. If he is eminent in any of the qualities which conduce
to his own good, he is, so far, a proper object of admiration. He
is so much the nearer to the ideal perfection of human nature.
If he is grossly deficient in those qualities, a sentiment the
opposite of admiration will follow. There is a degree of folly, and
a degree of what may be called (though the phrase is not un-
90 objectionable) lowness or depravation of taste, which, though it
cannot justify doing harm to the person who manifests it,
renders him necessarily and properly a subject of distaste, or, in
extreme cases, even of contempt: a person could not have the
opposite qualities in due strength without entertaining these
feelings. Though doing no wrong to anyone, a person may so
act as to compel us to judge him, and feel him, as a fool, or as
a being of an inferior order: and since this judgment and feeling
are a fact which he would prefer to avoid, it is doing him a
service to warn him of it beforehand, as of any other disagree-
100 able consequence to which he exposes himself. It would be well,
indeed, if this good office were much more freely rendered than
the common notions of politeness at present permit, and if one
person could honestly point out to another that he thinks him
in fault, without being considered unmannerly or presuming.
We have a right, also, in various ways, to act upon our

unfavourable opinion of any one, not to the oppression of his
individuality, but in the exercise of ours. We are not bound, for
example, to seek his society; we have a right to avoid it (though
not to parade the avoidance), for we have a right to choose the
110 society most acceptable to us. We have a right, and it may be
our duty, to caution others against him, if we think his example
or conversation likely to have a pernicious effect on those with
whom he associates. We may give others a preference over
him in optional good offices, except those which tend to his
improvement. In these various modes a person may suffer very
severe penalties at the hands of others, for faults which directly
concern only himself; but he suffers these penalties only in so
far as they are the natural, and, as it were, the spontaneous consequences of the faults themselves, not because they are pur-
120 posely inflicted on him for the sake of punishment. A person
who shows rashness, obstinacy, self-conceit – who cannot live
within moderate means – who cannot restrain himself from
hurtful indulgences – who pursues animal pleasures at the expense of those of feeling and intellect – must expect to be
lowered in the opinion of others, and to have a less share of
their favourable sentiments; but of this he has no right to complain, unless he has merited their favour by special excellence in
his social relations, and has thus established a title to their good
offices, which is not affected by his demerits towards himself.

A *Paragraph 1*

57 *That which should lead us to consider other members of society is*

    (*a*) moral duty (*b*) a sense of obligation (*c*) a social contract
    (*d*) a grateful heart (*e*) natural law

15 *'Rights' are established by*

    (*a*) conduct (*b*) the interests of others (*c*) law (*d*) convention
    (*e*) law and convention

104 *'Fixed on some equitable principle' (line 11) means*

    (*a*) fairly decided
    (*b*) arranged so that shares are equal
    (*c*) controlled by an arbitrator
    (*d*) paid for by a capital levy
    (*e*) settled by calm discussion

32 'The labours and sacrifices' (*line 11*) *could* not *include*

(*a*) taxes (*b*) fines (*c*) military service (*d*) jury service (*e*) assisting the police

50 *The preposition* 'to' *in the sentence beginning* 'These conditions . . . (line 13) shows that the last six words of the sentence are linked with the word*

(*a*) conditions (*b*) justified (*c*) enforcing (*d*) costs (*e*) none of these

69 'At all costs' (*line 14*) *means*

(*a*) however violently
(*b*) whatever the expense
(*c*) however great the damage to society
(*d*) however much some individual liberty suffers
(*e*) to prevent anarchy

78 *If a separate paragraph were made of the last part of this paragraph, where should it begin?*

(*a*) 'Nor is this all . . .' (*line 15*)
(*b*) 'The acts . . .' (*line 15*)
(*c*) 'The offender . . .' (*line 18*)
(*d*) 'As soon as . . .' (*line 19*)
(*e*) 'But there is no room . . . '(*line 23*)

9 'Punished by opinion' (*line 19*) *means*

(*a*) condemned by a vote
(*b*) looked down on
(*c*) restrained by common consent
(*d*) arbitrarily punished
(*e*) found guilty but released

53 'The question . . . becomes open to discussion' (*lines 21–23*)

(*a*) because there are now clearly two sides to the question
(*b*) because of the possibility of private vengeance
(*c*) because a wrong must be righted
(*d*) because interference may do harm all round
(*e*) because interference is now justifiable

103 'Social (*as opposed to* 'legal') freedom' (*line 28*) *should be denied to the man who*

(*a*) injures another man's interests
(*b*) fails to bear his share of labours and sacrifices.

(*c*) withholds fulfilment

(*d*) fails in consideration for someone, without infringing his rights

(*e*) promotes the general welfare

19 *The writer's prime concern in this paragraph is for*

(*a*) the good of society

(*b*) the good of the individual

(*c*) the rights of society

(*d*) the rights of individuals

(*e*) moral codes

B *Rewrite the first paragraph not in general but in particular terms, giving examples which will fit each point that the writer is making.*

C *Set out (50–100 words each) the arguments of the second and third paragraphs.*

D *How far do these last two paragraphs modify what has been said in the first paragraph? Are there any places where they seem to you to be inconsistent with the first paragraph?*

E *What would be Mill's view about the attitude society should adopt to suicide? To adultery? To homosexuality between adults? To drunkenness? To speeding in a built-up area? To obstructive parking? Do our present laws agree with him? Do you agree with him?*

II

† *Two Concepts of Liberty*, by Isaiah Berlin, 1958

I am normally said to be free to the degree to which no human being interferes with my activity. Political liberty in this sense is simply the area within which a man can do what he might want. If I am prevented by other persons from doing what I might want I am to that degree unfree; and if the area within which I can do what I might want is contracted by other men beyond a certain minimum, I can be described as being coerced, or, it may be, enslaved. Coercion is not, however, a term that covers every

form of inability. If I say that I am unable to jump more than
ten feet in the air, or cannot read because I am blind, or cannot
understand the darker pages of Hegel, it would be eccentric to
say that I am to that degree enslaved or coerced. Coercion implies the deliberate interference of other human beings within the
area in which I wish to act. You lack political liberty or freedom
only if you are prevented from attaining your goal by human
beings. Mere incapacity to attain your goal is not lack of political freedom. This is brought out by the use of such modern
expressions as 'economic freedom' and its counterpart, 'economic slavery'. It is argued, very plausibly, that if a man is too
poor to afford something on which there is no legal ban – a loaf
of bread, a journey round the world, recourse to the law courts –
he is as little free to have it as he would be if it were forbidden
him by law. If my poverty were a kind of disease, which prevented me from buying bread or paying for the journey round
the world, or getting my case heard, as lameness prevents me
from running, this inability would not naturally be described as
a lack of freedom at all, least of all political freedom. It is only
because I believe that my inability to get what I want is due to
the fact that other human beings have made arrangements
whereby I am, whereas others are not, prevented from having
enough money with which to pay for it, that I think myself a
victim of coercion or slavery. In other words, this use of the
term depends on a particular social and economic theory about
the causes of my poverty or weakness. If my lack of means is due
to my lack of mental or physical capacity, then I begin to speak
of being deprived of freedom (and not simply of poverty) only if
I accept the theory. If, in addition, I believe that I am being
kept in want by a definite arrangement which I consider unjust
or unfair, I speak of economic slavery or oppression. 'The nature
of things does not madden us, only ill will does', said Rousseau.
The criterion of oppression is the part that I believe to be played
by other human beings, directly or indirectly, in frustrating my
wishes. By being free in this sense I mean not being interfered
with by others. The wider the area of non-interference the
wider my freedom.

This is certainly what the classical English political philosophers meant when they used this word. They disagreed about
how wide the area could or should be. They supposed that it

could not, as things were, be unlimited, because if it were, it
50 would entail a state in which all men could boundlessly interfere with all other men; and this kind of 'natural' freedom would
lead to social chaos in which men's minimum needs would not
be satisfied; or else the liberties of the weak would be suppressed by the strong. Because they perceived that human purposes and activities do not automatically harmonize with one
another; and, because (whatever their official doctrines) they
put high value on other goals, such as justice, or happiness, or
security, or varying degrees of equality, they were prepared to
curtail freedom in the interest of other values and, indeed, of
60 freedom itself. For, without this, it was impossible to create the
kind of association that they thought desirable. Consequently, it
is assumed by these thinkers that the area of men's free action
must be limited by law. But equally it is assumed, especially by
such libertarians as Locke and Mill in England, and Constant
and Tocqueville in France, that there ought to exist a certain
minimum area of personal freedom which must on no account
be violated, for if it is overstepped, the individual will find
himself in an area too narrow for even that minimum development of his natural faculties which alone makes it possible to
70 pursue, and even to conceive, the various ends which men hold
good or right or sacred. It follows that a frontier must be drawn
between the area of private life and that of public authority.
Where it is to be drawn is a matter of argument, indeed of
haggling. Men are largely interdependent, and no man's
activity is so completely private as never to obstruct the lives of
others in any way. 'Freedom for the pike is death for the minnows'; the liberty of some must depend on the restraint of
others. Still, a practical compromise has to be found.

.   .   .

What made the protection of individual liberty so sacred to
80 Mill? In his famous essay he declared that unless men are left
to live as they wish 'in the path which merely concerns themselves', civilization cannot advance; the truth will not, for lack
of a free market in ideas, come to light; there will be no scope
for spontaneity, originality, genius, for mental energy, for
moral courage. Society will be crushed by the weight of 'collective mediocrity'. Whatever is rich and diversified will be crushed

by the weight of custom, by men's constant tendency to conformity, which breeds only 'withered capacities', 'pinched and
hidebound', 'cramped and warped' human beings. 'Pagan
90 self-assertion is as worthy as Christian self-denial.' 'All the
errors which a man is likely to commit against advice and warning are far outweighed by the evil of allowing others to constrain
him to what they deem is good.' The defence of liberty consists
in the 'negative' goal of warding off interference. To threaten a
man with persecution unless he submits to a life in which he
exercises no choices of his goals, to block before him every door
but one, no matter how noble the prospect upon which it opens,
or how benevolent the motives of those who arrange this, is to
sin against the truth that he is a man, a being with a life of his
100 own to live. This is liberty as it has been conceived by liberals
in the modern world from the days of Erasmus (some would say
of Occam) to our own. Every plea for civil liberties and individual rights, every protest against exploitation and humiliation,
against the encroachment of public authority, or the mass
hypnosis of custom or organized propaganda, springs from this
individualistic, and much disputed, conception of man.

Three facts about this position may be noted. In the first
place Mill confuses two distinct notions. One is that all coercion
is, in so far as it frustrates human desires, bad as such, although
110 it may have to be applied to prevent other, greater evils; while
non-interference, which is the opposite of coercion, is good as
such, although it is not the only good. This is the 'negative'
conception of liberty in its classical form. The other is that men
should seek to discover the truth, or to develop a certain type
of character of which Mill approved – fearless, original, imaginative, independent, non-conforming to the point of eccentricity,
and so on – and that truth can be found, and such character can
be bred, only in conditions of freedom. Both these are liberal
views, but they are not identical, and the connexion between
120 them is, at best, empirical. No one would argue that truth or
freedom or self-expression could flourish where dogma crushes
all thought. But the evidence of history tends to show (as,
indeed, was argued by James Stephen in his formidable attack
on Mill in his Liberty, Equality, Fraternity) that integrity,
love of truth and fiery individualism grow at least as often in
severely disciplined communities among, for example, the

puritan Calvinists of Scotland or New England, or under military discipline, as in more tolerant or indifferent societies; and if this is so accepted, Mill's argument for liberty as a necessary
130 condition for the growth of human genius falls to the ground. If his two goals proved incompatible, Mill would be faced with a cruel dilemma, quite apart from the further difficulties created by the inconsistency of his doctrines with strict utilitarianism, even in his own humane version of it.

In the second place, the doctrine is comparatively modern. There seems to be scarcely any consciousness of individual liberty as a political ideal in the ancient world. Condorcet has already remarked that the notion of individual rights is absent from the legal conceptions of the Romans and Greeks; this seems
140 to hold equally of the Jewish, Chinese, and all other ancient civilizations that have since come to light. The domination of this ideal has been the exception rather than the rule, even in the recent history of the West. Nor has liberty in this sense often formed a rallying cry for the great masses of mankind. The desire not to be impinged upon, to be left to oneself, has been a mark of high civilization both on the part of individuals and communities. The sense of privacy itself, of the area of personal relationships as something sacred in its own right, derives from a conception of freedom which, for all its religious roots, is
150 scarcely older, in its developed state, than the Renaissance or the Reformation. Yet its decline would mark the death of a civilization, of an entire moral outlook.

The third characteristic of this notion of liberty is of greater importance. It is that liberty in this sense is not incompatible with some kinds of autocracy, or at any rate with the absence of self-government. Liberty in this sense is principally concerned with the area of control, not with its source. Just as a democracy may, in fact, deprive the individual citizen of a great many liberties which he might have in some other form of society, so
160 it is perfectly conceivable that a liberal-minded despot would allow his subjects a large measure of personal freedom. The despot who leaves his subjects a wide area of liberty may be unjust, or encourage the wildest inequalities, care little for order, or virtue, or knowledge, but provided he does not curb their liberty, or at least curbs it less than many other régimes, he meets with Mill's specification. Freedom in this sense is not,

at any rate logically, connected with democracy or self-government. Self-government may, on the whole, provide a better
guarantee of the preservation of civil liberties than other
170 régimes, and has been defended as such by libertarians. But
there is no necessary connexion between individual liberty and
democratic rule. The answer to the question 'Who governs
me?' is logically distinct from the question 'How far does
government interfere with me?' It is in this difference that the
great contrast between the two concepts of negative and positive
liberty, in the end, consists. For the 'positive' sense of liberty
comes to light if we try to answer the question, not 'What am
I free to do or be?', but 'By whom am I ruled?' or 'Who is to
say what I am, and what I am not, to be or do?' The connexion
180 between democracy and individual liberty is a good deal more
tenuous than it seemed to many advocates of both. The desire
to be governed by myself, or at any rate to participate in the
process by which my life is to be controlled, may be as deep a
wish as that of a free area for action, and perhaps historically
older. But it is not a desire for the same thing. So different is it,
indeed, as to have led in the end to the great clash of ideologies
that dominates our world. For it is this – the 'positive' conception of liberty: not freedom from, but freedom to – which the
adherents of the 'negative' notion represent as being, at times,
190 used as a specious disguise for brutal tyranny.

F *Choose the most suitable words to fill the gaps in this summary of the
first paragraph.*

It is only possible to say that a man is — 97 [free/coerced/
perverted/contracted] if he is restrained by — 55 [political
liberty/other people/blindness/inability]; but if some — 24
[inherent/mental/special/eccentric] limitation prevents him
from doing something, we must describe this as — 85 [coercion/
inability/slavery/incapacity] rather than lack of freedom. The
phrase 'economic slavery' therefore — 36 [argues/implies/
proves/indicates] that a man, though not coerced by — 94
[nature/lameness/politics/law], is in effect a slave because of —
12 [indirect/obvious/contrived/unfair] pressures upon him for
which — 39 [doctors/lawyers/economists/men] are — 65 [plainly/
ultimately/directly/secretly] responsible. No one can claim that
he lacks freedom, — 46 [however/moreover/therefore/neverthe-

less], unless he — **80** [subscribes to/propounds/denies/acquiesces] a theory which — **31** [appoints/assigns/allows/adapts] to his inabilities an origin that is — **88** [outside human control/under human control/just/unjust]. Beyond this, he will describe a — **42** [decisive/human/controllable/specific] — **99** [limitation/ill will/control/exploitation] of his freedom by others as slavery or oppression.

G *Suggest concrete examples (such as might apply in a school or a family) of*
1. 'natural' freedom leading to social chaos *(line 51)*
2. the liberties of the weak being suppressed by the strong *(line 53)*
3. human purposes and activities not automatically harmonizing with each other *(line 54)*
4. curtailing freedom in the interest of freedom itself *(line 59)*
5. a minimum area of personal freedom which must on no account be violated *(line 66)*
6. a frontier drawn between the area of private life and that of public authority *(line 71)*
7. a practical compromise between 'freedom for the pike' and 'death for the minnows' *(lines 76-78)*

H *Re-read the last three paragraphs. Then shut the book, and explain in your own words the three points which the writer makes about Mill's position.*

I *In a footnote to this essay the writer discusses the question whether a man can be said to have acted freely, in any sense, if he betrays a friend under the threat of torture. What are your views on this?*

J 'The encroachment of public authority, the mass hypnosis of custom or organized propaganda' *(line 104)*. *Which offers the greater threat to liberty, a bureaucracy that interferes with individuals to prevent the weak from going to the wall, or a government that encourages business interests to be 'hidden persuaders'? Discuss this.*

K 'There is no necessary connection between individual liberty and democratic rule' *(line 171)*. *Discuss this point further.*

III

† *Glaucon*, by M. V. C. Jeffreys, 1955

The central problem of social life, as it presents itself to the individual and to the community, is how to reconcile these rival claims of self and society. A practical *modus vivendi* can usually be achieved by compromise; each individual agrees to concede certain rights to his fellows in order to induce them to make the like concessions to him. Duties are a *quid pro quo* for rights. In this way the individual is assured of a limited freedom and of adequate protection, and the community is assured of sufficient cohesion and stability while retaining enough variety and
10 initiative within it to give it vitality. This sort of implicit social contract, which is the basis of every existing political community, allows of very great elasticity between extremes. But there are limits beyond which the system breaks down. Individual variety and initiative may be greater than the community can hold together in unity; the community will then disintegrate as the city states of the ancient world. Or the central power may impose itself so firmly, in the manner of an eastern despotism, that revolt is provoked or else initiative dies and the state becomes fossilized. In one case there is explosion; in the other
20 desiccation. A good working test of the health of a community, as was suggested in another connection, is the power to contain maximum variety within unity.

Although this practical balance of freedom and control is the way in which the situation is in fact met by actual societies it is no real solution of the problem. It is no solution because it does not transcend the antithesis which gives rise to the problem; it only strikes a balance between the opposite poles of the antithesis. So far from being a solution, the usual working compromise between the claims of the individual and the claims of
30 society is only a way of avoiding a solution.

At the philosophical level there are three possible answers to the problem of the rival claims of individual and society.

(i) We can say that the claim of the individual is alone valid. Self-interest is the only standard of conduct. If, as the Utilitarians maintained, the result of the universal pursuit of self-interest is in fact the welfare of all, well and good; but in any case there is no higher authority than self-interest.

(ii) We can say that the claim of society is alone valid. The state, as Aristotle said, is prior to the individual, who depends
40 upon it for his very existence and owes it his total service. In its modern forms this doctrine likes to dramatize itself, as in the Hegelian mysticism of the state as a super-soul or the Marxian apocalypse of a new earth after the historical catastrophe.

Before going on to the third possible answer we ought to recognize that the terms 'individual' and 'society', which we have been using, are abstractions, often convenient but always treacherous. We are accustomed to the conventional picture of a hypothetical 'individual' moving, like an actor on a stage, in front of a drop-scene called 'society'. Neither individual nor
50 society exists in that sense. Individuals are neither separate nor self-sufficient. Society is neither a mere sum of individuals nor is it a super-ego, but is a complex of relationships of a kind to which the term 'personal' is appropriate as indicating both the rational and moral nature of the association and also the fact that full human life is possible only in community.

(iii) The third philosophical position is that both sides of the paradox (the claim of the individual and the claim of the community) are valid, and the tension between them must be resolved by being transcended. This would be accomplished –
60 theoretically – if we could find a principle that reconciles freedom and service; for the service that is perfect freedom would satisfy the claims of community and individual at the same time, since the individual would be able to fulfil himself in and through service to the community.

Freedom, it must be noted, is a positive thing—the achievement of something (i.e. the best of which one is capable) and not only the absence of something (i.e. restraint). It is true that absence of restraint is a necessary condition of freedom. But it is important not to confuse the conditions of freedom with free-
70 dom itself. We have already seen that the most fatal restraint from which we need to be liberated as a first condition of the achievement of freedom in a positive sense is the inhibition of self-love – i.e. anxiety and concern about one's own safety, comfort, or reputation. Without liberation from self, all other

liberty is no more than a self-indulgent and ultimately frustrating escape from responsibility. One of the great weaknesses of our western liberal democracy is that its idea of freedom is of this negative sort. As the former President of the University of Chicago put it not long ago: 'Our great preoccupation to-day
80 is freedom. When we talk about freedom we usually mean freedom from something. Freedom of the press is freedom from censorship. . . . Freedom of thought is freedom from thinking. Freedom of worship is freedom from religion.'

We begin to approach true freedom in proportion as we lose ourselves in something greater than ourselves. We may expect, that is to say, to find freedom in service. But, while human experience at large endorses the paradox that service is freedom, it also clearly warns us that not any or every kind of service is liberating. The question therefore is: What kind of service is
90 freedom? Or: What is the nature of the relationship in which service is freedom? Now it is clear that this relationship is what (to give it its best and shortest name) we know as love. We know, from our own experience and from innumerable examples from history and everyday life around us, that devoted service liberates and fosters personal growth where unwilling service does not. But, having said that, we must obviously go farther. It is not enough to look at the situation one-sidedly. We have to ask not only whether the citizen, disciple, or devotee gives his service in love, but whether he himself is loved – that is, whether
100 the person or institution he serves treats him as an end in himself and of infinite value as a human soul, or only as material or an instrument. If the latter, his devotion is misdirected and he will be destroyed like the moth in the flame. Not only that, but the person or institution served will ultimately destroy itself by accepting such service, since nothing is left in the end but ashes; the State that devours its citizens cannot be a community. Only when the love relationship is, in modern jargon, bilateral is service really freedom, and the self given without reserve is given back fulfilled to the giver. That is the nature of love. And
110 because that is the nature of love, it is a law of life that persons grow to full stature by giving, not by getting.

It follows therefore that the conditions of true freedom and also of true community are to be found in the context of the love relationship. It follows also that the key to true community is to be found in the meaning of the personal, since love is the essentially personal relationship. Love might in fact be defined as the relationship that treats people as persons – i.e. treats them as sacred. It is love that *constitutes* the personal: it is through loving and being loved that persons grow as persons.

120   The love relationship, though sometimes approached as between two or among a few persons, is never found in actual life except imperfectly. Institutions and associations do not love; for the most part institutions are not expressions of love so much as protective devices designed to make up for man's lack of love. We need the morality of law to supply the lack of a morality of love. But it is well that the morality of law should know its imperfection, for there is then some chance that love may work like leaven to redeem the morality of law.

But some institutions are more compatible than others with
130 the principle of love. That is to say, some institutions do more to safeguard the ultimate sacredness of the individual human soul and go to utmost limits to protect minorities within a common life, while others ruthlessly exploit their human material in the interests of the line of policy determined by the group that holds power.

If this exposition is sound, we have arrived at the theoretical solution of the dilemma presented by the rival claims of individual and community, and we have arrived at it by nothing more sensational than the recognition of a truth constantly
140 delivered through common human experience. It would seem that nothing remains except for mankind, in the clear light of reason, to make the command 'Love one another' the foundation-stone of social life and proceed to build upon it. It is notable, however, that after six thousand years of civilized history, man still fails to achieve the community of love, evident as is its charm, not to say expediency. Human beings continue to precipitate themselves into ever larger and more terrible catastrophes rather than treat one another decently. This persistent sinning against the light suggests on the face of it that
150 virtue is not, as Socrates maintained in the *Protagoras*, a function of reason, but that, in the language of the Collect for the First Sunday after Epiphany, it is one thing 'to perceive and know what things we ought to do', but another thing to 'have grace and power faithfully to fulfil the same'.

It was said a little earlier that persons grow as persons by loving and being loved. Paradoxical as it may seem, the 'being loved' is in an important sense prior to the 'loving'. In other words, man needs redemption. The paradox becomes clearer if we ask: Why cannot man resolve his central dilemma of his own
160 volition, in the light of reason? Animals do so by instinct. Why does man make such a mess of it with his superior equipment? The answer is that man makes a mess of it *because* of his superior equipment. For animals, conflict is resolved by the adjustment of exterior relations. For man the conflict remains in the soul. The reason for this is clear. The two fundamental urges that need reconciliation – (whether, with Freud, we label them self and sex, or separation and union, getting and giving) – these two urges come into irreconcilable conflict when they become *conscious*. At the level of consciousness self-love is born.
170 When some other impulse comes into conflict with the urge to self-preservation, man *knows* it. Instead of the animals' emergency machinery of self-preservation man has a sentiment of self-interest which makes him anxious when he ought to be bold, greedy when he ought to be generous, which in other words makes him constantly mindful of self when effective action demands that he should forget self. It is thus man's self-conscious reason which creates man's central problem. Man is justly crowned Lord of Creation, but his crown is a crown of thorns, pricking blood all the time from his brow.
180 There are three recognized ways in which the inhibition of self-concern can be broken and the constrained power liberated. One is the violent stimulation, at instinctive level, of some great primary urge, such as the mother's urge to defend her young, so that it temporarily overwhelms everything else and dominates the situation. The second is Dutch courage – i.e. the anaesthetization of the higher centres by something like alcohol so that the person becomes an extreme extrovert. Under the influence of drink we are able to forget ourselves literally as well as metaphorically. The remaining means is the condition in which a
190 person's whole being is so claimed and taken possession of by some supreme enthusiasm that concern about self is lost in devotion to the object. It is obvious that this third alternative is the only one of the three which, by accomplishing the reorientation of the person as a whole, offers a solution at a mature

level. But – and this is very important – the object of devotion must irresistibly appeal to the person. Notwithstanding the legend of Pygmalion one cannot create or constitute the object of devotion and then decide to be swept off one's feet by it. One must be taken out of oneself and lose oneself. It is in this sense 200 that the 'being loved' is prior to the 'loving', and that man needs to be redeemed.

L *Read lines 1 to 43 carefully, and then sort out the following words into four groups, by placing*

(a) *against words which refer to the claims of self,*

(b) *against words which refer to the claims of society,*

(c) *against words which refer to the reconciliation of these two claims,*

(d) *against words which refer to the result of failure to reconcile the two claims*

4 cohesion (*line 9*), 81 community (*line 2*), 37 compromise (*line 4*), 105 control (*line 23*), 26 desiccation (*line 20*), 62 disintegration (*line 15*), 30 duties (*line 6*), 74 elasticity (*line 12*), 2 explosion (*line 19*), 71 fossilization (*line 19*), 33 freedom (*line 23*), 102 individual (*line 2*), 16 Marxism (*line 42*), 60 modus vivendi (*line 3*), 100 protection (*line 8*), 83 revolt (*line 18*), 13 rights (*line 5*), 67 service (*line 40*), 25 social contract (*line 10*), 76 stability (*line 9*), 8 striking a balance (*line 27*), 47 transcending the antithesis (*line 26*), 89 unity (*line 15*), 20 Utilitarianism (*line 34*). 51 *Why are the words* 'initiative' *and* 'variety' *not included in this list?*

M *It is possible to illustrate the point made in lines 65–83 in simple visual terms, by referring to the difference between a weather-vane and a compass. Write a short talk, using this illustration, to convey the ideas in this paragraph to someone younger than yourself.*

N *Here is a summary of the argument of the next four paragraphs (lines 84–135). Below it are the words required to fill the blanks appropriately (and a few more besides). Choose the right word for each blank, and use no word twice.*

If freedom is to be — **96**, a man must be freed even from the demands of — **5**: he must lose himself in — **17**. Yet — **72** of this kind cannot result from — **49** service; nor is it found when the — **1** treats the service it receives as more — **91** than the — **34** who gives it. In other words, there must be — **58** on both sides if service is to be freedom; — **64** must replace — **29** as the central activity of life, if the community and the — **84** are to have a common — **68** rather than — **40** interests. When therefore we seek a — **61** rather than a — **11**, our problem moves from the — **52** to the — **77** level; yet this does not mean that institutions cease to interest us, since law, though it is — **21** by — **86** with love, can both afford some — **43** when love is — **7** and also provide better — **92** in which love may grow.

(*Nouns*)

community, comparison, compromise, conditions, getting, giving, goal, growing, individual, liberation, love, material, morality, person, protection, relationship, self, service, solution

(*Adjectives*)

bilateral, common, conflicting, human, imperfect, important, lacking, legal, personal, positive, unwilling

O *Summarize the argument of the last three paragraphs in your own words.*

P *Suggest a heading (3–9 words) for each paragraph in this extract.*

Q *This passage presents the Christian doctrine of man as something which an intelligent observer could deduce from a study of human behaviour and human problems. Do you find this convincing? If you do, criticize the passage of Mill from Jeffreys's viewpoint. If you do not, criticize the passage of Jeffreys from Mill's viewpoint.*

R *(Berlin, lines 48–61; Jeffreys, lines 65–76)*

In what ways is a wild animal more free or less free than you are? Is it true that by submitting to disciplines (e.g. learning) one can become more free? Does recent knowledge of the effects of heredity and environment affect your answer?

SOCIETY AND THE INDIVIDUAL

S *Discuss the rules (written and unwritten) which apply in your school, with reference to Berlin, lines 79–106, and Jeffreys, lines 120–135.*

T *Discuss the following remark, made to a committee by an intelligent but critical witness, with reference to Jeffreys, lines 180–201*

'The people whom I meet in the suburbs of the great city in which I work, even the products of grammar school fifth forms, show some very real deficiencies: an incapacity for objective reasoning; a reliance on three basic principles: "What I like is beautiful; what I think is right; what I do is good"; an incapacity for awe or reverence before the natural world or before persons; an inability to relax, to have leisure in the biblical sense of "being still", or to reflect upon their lives; and an incapacity for creative suffering, despite much pain and anxiety. The people who are most likely to get "lit up" are those who have a firm hold on some "end" of man – whether Marxist, Christian or other.'

U *Write an essay on* Society and the Individual
or What is Freedom?
or The difference between a crime and a sin
or Man's dilemma
or Law and love.

Appendix

Some Problems and Exercises

Most of the questions in this book are included as an encouragement to you to read carefully, to use evidence, and to draw legitimate conclusions. Studying a writer's work in this way makes demands on your intelligence and your concentration – whereas guessing the point he is making, without regard to logic or to the clues he has dropped, is as easy as it is unrewarding.

You may care now to practise these skills on some 'inferential problems'. They have no literary merit, but they provide a concentrated exercise in reading closely what you are told and making deductions patiently from it.

A 1 Five men, born in successive years, all have birthdays on December 1st. But their joint celebration turned into a quarrel last year, and before the evening was out each of them had hit one of the others. Luckily no two men chose the same victim.

I went to see all five, while they were still nursing their injuries, and got the following information:

ANTON: The man I hit is a year younger than I am, and he hit Boris.

BORIS: I am not the youngest of these five men; I am thirty-four.

CARLOS: The man who hit me is a year younger than Daniel and is the man whom Daniel hit.

DANIEL: No two men hit each other. Boris hit a man older than himself.

ENRICO: I did not hit the man who hit the man who hit the man who hit the man who hit me. The oldest of us five is lying.

I later discovered that both of the things which one man had told me were untrue, but that all other statements were correct.

Who is the oldest of these five men? How old is he? Whom did he hit?

B 3 The four boats, 'Alderney', 'Guernsey', 'Herm', and 'Sark', are based on these four islands, and also have skippers who bear the same four names; but luckily no skipper has the same name as his boat or his base, and no boat is based on the island which shares its name. Mr Herm's boat has the same name as the skipper who is based on Herm – who, incidentally, is not Mr Alderney, a man whom everyone calls John.

The owner of this fleet unfortunately uses each of the four names without making it clear whether he is referring to the skipper, the boat, or the base – and often changes from one practice to another in mid-sentence. Recently, when every skipper was aboard his own boat, and every boat was alongside at its home base, he sent a telegram to the local manager of the fleet: 'Transfer nets from Sark to Alderney by fast launch.'

Though the owner could not be referring to Mr Alderney (since he always calls him John), this telegram had four possible meanings for the local manager.

Which boat is based on Guernsey and who is its skipper?

C 5 Mr North, Mr East, Mr South and Mr West recently played three rubbers of bridge, cutting for partners before each rubber. In the course of the three rubbers it so happened that each man occupied the three positions which do not correspond with his own name.

Mr East was five shillings up when he moved from position W to position N; but he lost even more money than Mr South did on the whole play.

Which rubber was the most profitable to those who won it? Who were they, and where were they sitting for this rubber?

Here are two more exercises, similar in type to those which you have met earlier in this book.

D 2 *The sentences printed below, when rearranged, form one coherent paragraph. Given that (a) is the first sentence, work out the right order.*

(a) History, it is said, is of no use; at least, a great critic, who is understood to have in the press a very elaborate work in that kind, not long since seemed to allege that writings of this sort did not establish a theory of the universe, and were therefore of no avail.

(b) What a gain if something would happen! Then one could describe it.

(c) Every day cannot be an era; a train of new speculation very often will not be found; and how dull it is to make it your business to write, to stay by yourself in a room to write, and then to have nothing to say!

(d) Not so; he was making history; Gibbon has written it down.

(e) But whatever may be the use of this sort of composition in itself and abstractedly, it is certainly of great use relatively and to literary men.

(f) Something has happened, and that something is history.

(g) He sits beside a library fire, with nice white paper, a good pen, a capital style, every means of saying everything, but nothing to say; of course he is an able man; of course he has an active intellect, besides wonderful culture; but still one cannot always have original ideas.

(h) On this account, since a sedate Greek discovered this plan for a grave immortality, a series of accomplished men have seldom been found wanting to derive a literary capital from their active and barbarous kindred.

(i) Consider the position of a man of that species.

(j) It is dreary work mending seven pens, and waiting for a theory to 'turn up'.

(k) Perhaps when a Visigoth broke a head, he thought that that was all.

APPENDIX

E 4 *In the following passage by T. H. Huxley, fourteen words have replaced those actually written. Deduce which these inappropriate words are, by means of their faulty logic or their ineptness, and say, if possible, what each actual word should be.*

Suppose it were perfectly certain that the life and fortune of every one of us would, one day or other, depend upon his winning or losing a game of chess. Don't you think that we should all consider it to be a primary step to learn at least the titles and the motions of the pieces; to have a notion of a gambit, and a keen eye for all the means of evading and getting out of check? Do you not think that we should look with a disapprobation amounting to suspicion, upon the father who ordered his son, or the state which authorized its members, to grow up without
10 knowing a pawn from a knight?

Therefore it is a very plain and elementary truth that the life, the fortune, and the happiness of every one of us, and, more or less, of those who are connected with us, do depend upon our knowing something of the rules of a game rather more difficult and complicated than chess. It is a game which has been played for several ages, every man and woman of us being one of the two players in a game of his and her own. The table is the world, the pieces are the phenomena of the universe, the rules of the game are what we call the laws of Nature. The
20 player on the other side is hidden from us. We know that his play is often fair, just, and patient. But also we know, to our cost, that he never condones a mistake, or makes the smallest allowance for ignorance. To the man who plays well, the highest compliments are paid, with that sort of overflowing generosity with which the strong shows delight in strength. And one who plays ill is checkmated – without haste, but without horror.

Answers

CHAPTERS 1–4 (pp. 1–20)

1 private **2** (*b*) **3** ? **4** (*c*) **5** advanced education, as opposed to mere literacy **6** (*e*) **7** ll. 3–5 **8** lively **9** (*d*) **10** abuses **11** 'or some of them'; 'modest'; the last sentence (notice especially the stress on 'still') **12** √ **13** (*d*) **14** The statement about Dickens: he wrote in the nineteenth century **15** (*a*) **16** popular taste **17** × **18** altruism **19** greed **20** (*a*) **21** (*b*) **22** fee-paying schools **23** (*a*) **24** ? **25** (*b*) **26** (*c*) **27** concern **28** justified **29** (*d*) **30** Mr Mabbott states that the equivalent is the *vote*. Can you see why? **31** (*c*) **32** √ **33** (*d*) **34** necessarily **35** (*d*) **36** (*c*) **37** exploited **38** compassion **39** (*a*) **40** (*a*) **41** ll. 40–43 **42** √ **43** (*d*) **44** pay **45** (*e*) **46** (*a*) **47** √ **48** ll. 28–30 **49** (*c*) **50** √ **51** (*a*) **52** (*a*) **53** (*c*) **54** decolonization; precolonial; westernization **55** (*c*) **56** (*b*) **57** (*c*) **58** exploitation (or hypochondriac) **59** given away **60** neglected **61** (*b*) **62** ? **63** (*c*) **64** alleviated **65** criterion **66** (*b*) **67** × **68** City livery companies or religious groups which have instituted schools **69** × **70** (*a*) **71** Impartial **72** (*d*) **73** (*c*) **74** (*b*) **75** √ **76** not esoteric **77** (*e*).

CHAPTERS 5–9 (pp. 21–55)

1 *A possible summary:*

Insurance (which can frivolously be described as betting) should come under government control. It is true that some people gain money – sometimes dishonestly – from insurance; but most people insure simply for the security it gives. Yet car insurance, being required by law, is in a special category, and gives the insurer great power. His action in refusing insurance to those who are 'accident prone' may be sensible, from the commercial point of view, but it is also unjust, for it treats individuals as types and may indeed punish people who have committed no offence. The Government, by making car insurance compulsory, provides much business for companies, and should demand, in return, that they standardize premiums and accept everyone legally permitted to drive. It should also, in other fields, set as the sum which companies must pay *either* the market value of what was lost *or* the amount for which it was insured – and not, as now, allow them to pay whichever of these two is the smaller. Thirdly, the Government should enforce prompt settlement of claims, with special arrangements for resolving points that are seriously disputed. It would be worth paying higher premiums for these improvements, since insurance exists to level out the unfairness of life, and should not itself be unfair.

2 modern   **3** (*b*)   **4** restrictions   **5** (*c*) – schemes   **6** (*c*)   **7** conflicts with   **8** conformity   **9** established   **10** province, as in 'the poultry-keeper's world'   **11** arbitrary   **12** (*b*) and (*e*)   **13** began   **14** re-adjust   **15** fossilize   **16** drivers likely to be involved in accidents   **17** corroborated   **18** people one meets outside one's home   **19** (*a*) and (*e*)   **20** (*a*)   **21** outlined   **22** temporary   **23** integral   **24** (*d*)   **25** perhaps 'majestic world' means 'the number of those men who are competing for military glory'   **26** on the whole, radical   **27** practical   **28** (*d*)   **29** (*a*)   **30** settled   **31** (*a*)   **32** illusory   **33** infringement   **34** separate   **35** asserted   **36** distinction   **37** postulated   **38** (*a*) and (*e*)   **39** meaning   **40** (*c*)   **41** intrinsic   **42** modern times   **43** overcame   **44** combination   **45** (*d*)   **46** (*c*)   **47** disconcerting   **48** (as in Ryle) all objects that man can perceive   **49** discomfort   **50** exploded   **51** (*e*)   **52** all people and all things; the lovers were so engrossed with each other that nothing and no-one else existed   **53** probably the same sense each time   **54** alternative   **55** evolved   **56** compulsory insurance of cars   **57** scale   **58** (*a*) (there are objective standards in everyday life and science, but not in history, etc.) and (*c*)   **59** familiar   **60** calculated   **61** 'How do you do?'   **62** rationalized   **63** worldliness: material pursuits   **64** (*d*)   **65** changing for dinner   **66** (*d*) – infinite   **67** startled   **68** spurious   **69** types of car insurance shown by statistics to be unremunerative   **70** concentrated   **71** qualifies   **72** much used   **73** expanded.

74 *A suggested summary for you to criticize:*

Hard though they are to distinguish, conventions and good manners differ in two ways: first, convention usually applies to public behaviour, and good manners to dealings between friends; secondly, good manners can be justified on the grounds that they are an attempt to set people at their ease. Unfortunately, good manners are apt to become antiquated and turn into meaningless and ridiculous conventions.

CHAPTERS 10–11 (pp. 56–80)

1 (*a*)   **2** belonged to   **3** understandable   **4** (*c*)   **5** (*b*)   **6** local
7 commune   **8** individuality   **9** growth   **10** absorbed into   **11** (*c*)
12 ll. 358–369   **13** relieve   **14** (*b*)   **15** (*c*)   **16** stressing   **17** evolution   **18** (*a*)   **19** at second hand   **20** garish   **21** (*c*)   **22** orderly
23 ll. 314–317   **24** slight   **25** craftsmanship   **26** (*b*)   **27** the book of
Isaiah: Christian thought about the death of Christ   **28** insulation
29 efficacious   **30** man   **31** ll. 318–324   **32** basically   **33** environment
34 therapeutic   **35** number   **36** engender   **37** (*a*)   **38** (*a*)   **39** (*d*)
40 vigorous humour   **41** initial   **42** 'secure and conventional Hebrew' (l. 92); 'If God … punishment' (ll. 310–314)   **43** (*a*)   **44** intimately
45 psychological   **46** superficial   **47** (*b*)   **48** (*d*)   **49** (*d*)
50 material   **51** forgotten   **52** fragility   **53** (*c*)   **54** blocked
55 ll. 234–261   **56** (*b*)   **57** an outcrop   **58** social   **50** impinge on
60 sound   **61** (*e*)   **62** challenge   **63** (*b*)   **64** palls   **65** no pretence
about   **66** liberated   **67** (*c*)   **68** primitive man: the Persians and Zoroastrians: Gnostics   **69** restricted   **70** secure   **71** (*b*)   **72** farm
73 (*c*)   **74** ll. 169–193   **75** latitude fifty north   **76** quality   **77** depreciate   **78** predominated   **79** assertive ('brassed on the board')
80 pilgrimage   **81** himself   **82** (*b*)   **83** conform   **84** (*b*)   **85** optimistic   **86** seasonal   **87** ll. 328–336   **88** impervious   **89** axiom
90 God   **91** superficially ornamental.

ANSWERS

CHAPTERS 12–14 (pp. 81–120)

1 After '. . . recent developments in physics' (l. 19). At this point Stebbing starts to look at the subject from the *writer's* point of view (rather than the reader's). First topic sentence: 'There is among common readers . . . findings' (ll. 13–16). Second topic sentence: 'Unfortunately, however, . . . discernment' (ll. 25–30) – and the next sentence repeats the idea more tersely. **2** (*a*) **3** (*e*) **4** function **5** (*b*) and (*c*) **6** (*b*) **7** Mendel **8** (*e*) **9** studies **10** (*d*) **11** 'Where there is universal free education for all children' **12** (*b*) **13** phenomenon (possibly 'regression') **14** (*c*) **15** skill in exposition: sympathy with laymen: realistic attitude to his own subject **16** heredity **17** 'You can plan . . . buildings' (ll. 56–58) and 'Parity of esteem . . . mockery' (ll. 59–61) **18** (*e*) **19** (*d*) **20** provision **21** (*a*) **22** (*g*) **23** (*d*) **24** (*a*) **25** (*c*) **26** 'tall' *or* 'small' **27** (*a*) and (*e*) **28** heredity **29** (*d*) **39** environment **31** (*a*) and (*f*); perhaps (*c*) **32** (*d*) **33** (*b*) **34** (*d*) **35** parents **36** attainment **37** (*a*) and (*c*) **38** brains **39** (*f*) **40** less than 80 per cent **41** (*a*) **42** (*a*) **43** equality **44** 'tall' *or* 'small' (the same as 26) **45** (*a*) and (*c*) **46** aptitude **47** (*f*) **48** (*d*) and (*e*) **49** (*d*) **50** intelligence **51** (*d*) **52** (*b*) **53** (*e*) **54** (*c*) **55** inheritance **56** (*b*) **57** (*b*) **58** (*a*) √ : (*b*) ? : (*c*) × : (*d*) √ : (*e*) √√ (or √) : (*f*) √ : (*g*) × : (*h*) ? : (*i*) √√ : (*j*) ? **59** (*b*) **60** disparity **61** (*c*) **62** intelligence **63** (*b*) **64** (*g*) **65** (*d*) **66** (*c*) **67** nature **68** regression **69** (*d*) **70** access **71** 'where there is education only for the privileged few' **72** somewhat sceptical ('Mammoth Guides to the Intelligent Man' suggests that readers are being both flattered and bullied: 'Guides through Chaos' implies that the blind lead the blind; the double negative of the main clause is ironic – amongst (or despite) all the shouting, the common reader *can* with difficulty learn something: the repetition of 'Guides' is perhaps ironic also).

8(ll196

CHAPTERS 15-17 (pp. 121-153)

1 Among the words discussed might well be: 'obviously'; 'rationalizations'; 'do not merit'; 'typical' (cf. 'old'); 'subject them'; 'long chairmanship' (suggests conservatism and senility); 'evidently'; 'felt' (rather than 'thought' – perhaps insignificant); 'duty to justify' (suggests closed minds); 'tried'; 'supreme object – punishment' 2 philistine   3 (b)   4 (c)   5 corporate   6 (e)   7 but   8 development   9 desert   10 (d)   11 (e)   12 (c) and (e)   13 display 14 misunderstandings   15 sympathy   16 or   17 (b)   18 unworthy 19 for   20 (a)   21 adapt   22 (d)   23 motive   24 (d)   25 extensive   26 resign   27 also   28 whether   29 status   30 immediate 31 rather   32 accumulation   33 offence   34 force   35 (d)   36 (d) 37 accounting   38 (a) and (d)   39 (f)   40 future   41 transmit 42 rebuff   43 in principle   44 record   45 however   46 (c) (does the writer *know* what an I.Q. is?)   47 thinkers   48 ignore   49 (c) (*and* to give shape to the argument)   50 (a)   51 'for' or 'indeed' 52 (b)   53 defined   54 (e)   55 legitimate   56 (e)   57 vary 58 right   59 impels   60 (a)   61 collate   62 (e)   63 associations 64 (b)   65 therefore   66 apologetically   67 (b)   68 justifies 69 nor   70 potential   71 affected   72 witticism   73 indeed 74 integral   75 condescended   76 (g) ('nasty, brutish, and short') 77 basis   78 (a)   79 biological   80 revenge   81 hence   82 stimulate   83 essence   84 but   85 developed   86 beyond.

CHAPTERS 18–19 (pp. 154–188)

1 community 2 (*d*) 3 (*b*) 4 (*b*) 5 self 6 disperse 7 lacking
8 (*c*) 9 (*b*) 10 appreciate 11 compromise 12 indirect 13 (*a*)
14 (*b*) 15 (*e*) 16 (*b*) 17 service 18 (*b*) 19 (*d*) 20 (*a*)
21 imperfect 22 Gothic 23 (*d*) 24 inherent 25 (*c*) 26 (*d*)
27 'practical and circumstantial difficulties of war', 'patriotism',
'difficulties of performance' are Lambert's own summaries 28 stimu-
lates a futile horror in the viewer 29 getting 30 (*b*) 31 assigns
32 (*b*) 33 (*a*) 34 person 35 falsify 36 implies 37 (*c*)
38 inessentials 39 men 40 conflicting 41 'society' (or 'sick')
42 specific 43 protection 44 (*b*) 45 (*a*) pretentious, stylized;
(*b*) meretricious, modish, tawdry; (*e*) austere, basic, functional, plain;
(*d*) jaded, prejudiced, submissive 46 therefore 47 (*c*) 48 moonlight 49 unwilling 50 (*d*) 51 because they, more than the other
words in this list, have a double reference – to the welfare both of
self and of society 52 legal 53 (*e*) 54 (*c*) 55 other people
56 'Red flag': much at the end of paragraph one; bomb throwing;
guillotining; barricades; war-horses? There are probably others
57 (*b*) 58 love 59 questioned 60 (*c*) 61 solution 62 (*d*)
63 (*a*) 64 giving 65 ultimately 66 certain key images 67 (*b*)
68 goal 69 (*d*) 70 vague abstractions 71 (*d*) 72 liberation
73 (*c*) 74 (*c*) 75 'the public' (see l. 7) 76 (*b*) 77 personal
78 (*e*) 79 advises 80 subscribes to 81 (*b*) 82 noble 83 (*d*)
84 individual 85 incapacity 86 comparison 87 disapproves of
88 under human control 89 (*b*) 90 analyse 91 important
92 conditions 93 sentimental 94 law 95 impatient with
96 positive 97 coerced 98 antiquated 99 limitation 100 (*a*)
101 (*c*) 102 (*a*) 103 (*d*) 104 (*a*) 105 (*b*) 106 'love' (rather
than 'sacrament') 107 (*a*).

APPENDIX

1 (*a*) If E is truthful, the 'chain' does not include all five men; instead, two men must have hit each other, and there was a 'chain' of three men.

But then D is lying; and either A or C (*both* of whom describe a 'chain' of three men) must be lying also.

∴ *E is not truthful, and the 'chain' does include all five men*

(*b*) Now (from A) $A \to x \to B$ ($\to$ = 'hits')

and (from C) $D \to y \to C$

∴ *Either* (i) $A \to D \to B \to C \to E \to A$

[and $A > D > B$ (> = 'is a year older than')]

Or (ii) $D \to A \to C \to B \to E \to D$

[and $D > A > C$]

∴ (from B and D) ages in (i) would be $C > A > D > B > E$

ages in (ii) would be $E > B > D > A > C$

(*c*) But if (ii) were correct, E's second statement would be true (which we know it is not).

∴ (i) is the correct possibility.

Carlos is the oldest; he is 37; he hit Enrico.

2 Walter Bagehot actually wrote the sentences in this order: (a), (e), (i), (g), (c), (j), (b), (f), (h), (k), (d).

3 If Mr Sark either skippers the 'Alderney' or is based on Alderney then *either* the 'Sark' is at Alderney or the 'Alderney' is at Sark (which will not fit in with the requirement about Mr Herm)

or the 'Sark' is *not* at Alderney and the 'Alderney' is *not* at Sark (but this produces five, rather than four, possible meanings).

∴ Mr Sark neither skippers the 'Alderney' nor is based on Alderney; and the possible meanings of the telegram can only be limited to four if the 'Sark' is based at Alderney *and* the 'Alderney' at Sark.

We thus get the pattern

Skipper	?	?	A	S
Boat	S	A	?	?
Base	A	S	?	?

We can now see that Mr Herm's boat must be the 'Sark', and Mr Sark must be based at Herm. Therefore the third column above must show Guernsey as the base, and the 'Herm' as the name of the boat.

Answer: The 'Herm', skippered by John Alderney.

4 *T. H. Huxley actually wrote*

Duty *not* step; names *not* titles; moves *not* motions; giving *not* evading; scorn *not* suspicion; allowed *not* ordered; allowed *not* authorized; yet *not* therefore; infinitely *not* rather; untold *not* several; chessboard *not* table; always *not* often; overlooks *not* condones; stakes *not* compliments; remorse *not* horror.

(If you changed 'his and her' to 'his or her', we think you are right; but Huxley wrote 'his and her'.)

5 *Partnership.* It is quickly seen that the players cannot have all three possible partnerships as well as move round the compass. Nor can they retain the same partners throughout, or else both losers would be down the same amount.

∴ There are 2 partnerships, 1 for two rubbers and 1 for one. Mr E must have been on the losing side in each partnership; Mr S must have been once on the losing and once on the winning side. *Who never partners Mr E at all?* Not Mr S (see above); not Mr W (since he cannot sit E both while Mr E sits N and while Mr E sits S). ∴ *Mr N.*

Now *if Mr E moves from W to N after the second rubber*, he sits S; W; N.

Then the man who partners him in the first rubber (sitting N) must sit E for the second rubber (since Mr N is then sitting S) and partner him again.

But this makes Mr E on the winning side for one partnership (five shillings up) and is therefore impossible.

So Mr E moves from W to N after the first rubber, and sits W; N; S; while Mr N sits S; EW; EW.

We now see that rubbers 1 and 3 must have been played with the same partnerships (since otherwise the man who partners Mr N for rubber 1 and Mr E for rubber 3 sits N both times) and we can fill in as follows

Player	1	2	3
Mr E	W	N	S
	win	lose	lose
Mr N	S	EW	EW
	lose	win	win
x	E	W	N
	win	win	lose
y	N	S	EW
	lose	lose	win

We immediately see that x is Mr S, and y is Mr W, and that Mr N's positions were S; E; W, and Mr W's positions were N; S; E.

As Mr S, who has twice beaten Mr W, is down at the end, the most profitable rubber was clearly *the third*: winners *Mr N (sitting W)* and *Mr W (sitting E)*.